The Right to Vegetarianism

Carlo Prisco

Hamilton Books

An Imprint of
Rowman & Littlefield
Lanham • Boulder • New York • Toronto • Plymouth, UK

Copyright © 2017 by Hamilton Books
4501 Forbes Boulevard, Suite 200, Lanham, Maryland 20706
Hamilton Books Acquisitions Department (301) 459-3366

Unit A, Whitacre Mews, 26-34 Stannary Street,
London SE11 4AB, United Kingdom

Library of Congress Control Number: 2016953903
ISBN: 978-0-7618-6866-8 (pbk : alk. paper)—ISBN: 978-0-7618-6867-5 (electronic)

∞™ The paper used in this publication meets the minimum requirements of American National Standard for Information Sciences Permanence of Paper for Printed Library Materials, ANSI/NISO Z39.48-1992.

Dedicated to all those who seek to defend their right

to live with respect for others . . . of any kind

Contents

Foreword

In the 1990s, Anna Charlton and I had a legal clinic at Rutgers University School of Law that involved cases that concerned animal issues. Although we called our enterprise the Rutgers Animal Rights Law Center, the reality is that animal did not then and do not know have any rights that are recognized by law. We represented humans who had legal rights and we argued that those rights required that the law respect our clients' views about animals.

For example, we represented students who did not want to use nonhuman animals as part of their coursework. We represented prisoners who wanted vegan food. In both cases, we argued that our human clients had constitutional rights to freedom of conscience that required schools and prisons to respect their choices. We called ourselves "animal rights lawyers," but we were really human rights lawyers who focused on situations where the exercise of those human rights involved nonhuman animals.

In this book, Carlo Prisco, the leading lawyer concerned with animal issues in Italy, comes to the conclusion that a right to vegetarian food (understood as food that contains no animal products) is one that cannot be grounded in animal rights because animals are property. They have no rights. Humans have rights, including the right to exploit their animal property. He argues that we must focus on human rights, including both constitutional and statutory rights, as a basis for a right to vegetarian food and he explores all the aspects and implications of such a right.

He also discusses the emergence of animal rights as a philosophical matter and he considers the status of animals within the law.

Prisco's writing is not based just on theory. In addition to being an academic who specializes in legal philosophy, he is a practicing lawyer who has had extensive experience dealing with these issues in real contexts. For example, in 2015, Prisco prevailed in an important case in which he successfully challenged a school district's requirement that a parental request for vegan food for a child had to be supported by certain health-related requirements that were not imposed on other children.

This book involves a fascinating mixture of theory and practice, and of philosophy and law. I look forward to Prisco's work as I am confident that he will emerge as a leading international figure in animal ethics and law. He's well on his way.

Gary L. Francione
Rutgers University School of Law
May 30, 2016

Introduction

First of all, a terminological clarification is needed: the term "vegetarianism" is not used here to distinguish what we usually call "vegetarianism" from "veganism," but in its original meaning, that is not (obviously!) "lacto-ovo vegetarianism," but, actually, any plant-based food, excluding all animal products.

The purpose of this work is to demonstrate the existence of the right of people to eat according to their ethical orientation. This orientation may lead them to eat lacto-ovo vegetarian, or vegan, or even fruitarian. The foundation of the protection is the same, and the underlying ethics refers to the respect toward nonhuman animals.

The concept of Animal rights is a modern one, born in what Norberto Bobbio called the "age of the rights," which was raised in the West in the twentieth century.

The animals referred to are, of course, nonhumans; international movements asked that we recognize the ownership of legal positions worthy of protection by the law for them.

The beginnings of the modern animal rights idea can be found everywhere in Western history, especially in ancient philosophy that, since the Orphic cults, attributed value to all beings, human or not, and sometimes even inanimate objects.

While it is impossible to speak about "animal rights" in ancient philosophy, what stands out is undoubtedly the principle of respect, that is a duty to refrain from harming humans and nonhumans.

Contemporary philosophy has taken up and developed some of the themes of the ancient philosophy, while some new were introduced, finally founding a philosophical and moral system that recognizes animal rights.

While, for the philosopher, it is "easy" to relate to the category of rights, extending it to nonhumans, the lawyer's way is likely to be more complex and difficult, as it will have to take into consideration the positive law.

The aim of this work is to analyze the most controversial aspects of the latest legal and philosophical currents on the subject, trying to approach them with a critical scrutiny to determine what is, or what could be, the state of the art.

Assuming that there is no legal system that includes animal rights, it is still possible to see an evolution of the Western laws from the initial consideration of nonhumans as mere property, to affirm certain obligations and restrictions regarding practices that involve animals.

The difficulties encountered by the law with nonhuman subjects lead, according to the animal rights philosophers, to a discrepancy or schizophrenia: the ratio legis seems to manifest considerations that are not reflected in a concrete way, or are contradicted by other laws, or limited in various ways.

While it could seem improbable, the rules relating to animals among Western countries are surprisingly similar, as similar as the ideological approaches.

The scope of this work will go beyond the limits and specificities of animal issues addressed in philosophy and those taken into account in the law, rather trying to combine the two disciplines in search of the lowest common denominator.

The main animal rights contemporary thinkers, despite the profound differences that separate them, believe that there cannot be any recognition of animal rights while they are used for food, and all of them agree that vegetarianism/veganism represents a moral imperative.

When philosophy comes to the food issue, it encounters (or clashes with) the most varied ideas, disciplines, circumstances, habits, and spiritual and religious beliefs. Without connecting all these elements together, it is impossible to make the philosophical precepts actual laws.

The food issue will be examined, beginning from the philosophical point of view, to legal questions, to help us understand how the contemporary law deals with it.

Arguing about the new challenges of the matter implies a step back to the origins. Where is it rooted? The question—as we know—is ancient and controversial, and it would be impossible to fully explore it in this work, but whoever is going to approach the issue will have to relate, at least in broad terms, with the main currents of thought about the foundation of rights.

Since the nature of human rights is controversial, obviously that of animals is more controversial—in both cases, the foundation and the actual application are controversial, though the animal rights debate is historically more limited than the other, which, involving the whole of society, may be considered coeval to it.

Through a reflection that is meant to represent the epitome of the main philosophical voices about animal rights, this work will consider the food issue as the lowest common denominator, since, despite significant differences, and even from various considerations (sometimes almost opposite), all animal rights theorists agree that the abolition of their use for human food purposes represents a moral obligation.

On the sidelines of all academic considerations there is the positive law that, in taking note of the interactions between humans and nonhumans, could not refrain from disciplining them in various ways. The jurist interested in understanding the legal regime of the relationships among species can address legislation, past and present, which, in the Western world, showed a static life for thousands of years, followed by the fast change in the contemporary law, more and more receptive to nonhuman subjects.

The comparative analysis of positive law will be necessary to verify the practical implications of the abovesaid philosophical theories, if indeed there were a way to do so.

Examining laws about nonhuman animals is also an opportunity to better understand the critical positions of those thinkers who, strongly contesting the current rules, call for a radical transformation of the legislative approach.

If it is true that philosophy agrees about the abolition of the use of nonhuman animals as food, it is also true that the law showed no receptivity in that and, indeed, it has shown its limits as a cultural expression of a society, which is able to give shape and binding to some instances, but that has to first pass through a process of cultural and social transformation.

Besides, the laws of a society represent a picture full of information and indices of the prevailing culture and expectations in relation to other associates and institutions: the picture, as said above, portrays a situation that has many more similarities rather than differences in the Western world.

While vegetarianism/veganism is the lowest common denominator of animal rights philosophy, no Western laws took it into account, but, recently, a sort of "vegetarianism issue" is rising in some legal systems.

This work stems from the consideration that there are social demands more and more frequent in connection with vegetarianism: those claims of a right could be called "right to vegetarianism."

If it is true that everyone is free to choose his or her own diet, it is also true that the realization of certain rights cannot be separated from the adoption of laws ensuring all the necessary precautions.

The final object of this work is to examine the first bill, concerning the discipline of an obligation to provide vegetarian and vegan alternatives to animal food.

The first attempt to regulate the vegetarian/vegan alternative in an organic and systematic way represents the first link between animal rights theories and positive law.

The question of the right to vegetarianism, or, rather, of its institutional-ization through the enactment of a law, raises many questions, in some ways opposite: Is it a legally founded claim? Or, on the contrary, would it be redundant with respect to current laws?

Chapter One

From Human Rights to Animal Rights

1.1 THE FUNDAMENT OF RIGHT

Bobbio and the Search for the Foundation of Right

One of the most controversial issues of the Western philosophy is the foundation of the concept of right: past the medieval theologies, many thinkers have tried to understand and justify the creation and application of right and of human rights.

The main dilemma is whether the right pre-exists in respects to mankind, or if the law-making activities of the associates is innovative and creative.

The search for the foundation of right could be crucial, reasoning of all those rights beyond human rights—which Attilio Pisanò has sharply defined as *dehumanized*[1] —are undoubtedly animal rights, environmental rights, etc.

Bobbio focused his attention on the foundation of right, considering and analyzing the main theories in his *L'età dei diritti* (*The Age of Rights*)[2] .

Before approaching the merits of the matter, the philosopher states three preliminary issues: i) what reason we should search for the foundation of right, ii) if we can find an absolute foundation, iii) whether it is desirable.

As to the first, it is necessary to distinguish whether the purpose of the research is to find the basis for a claim of something already owned, or for something that is intended to be achieved. Therefore, in one case, it will be necessary to examine the law in force, to find its source, while, in the other case, we must strive to achieve social sharing and recognition by the legislature.

According to Bobbio, the persuasion of the existence of an absolute foundation of right (second question) would arise as a result of the action of persuasion. The proponents of new rights would reach to believe that their arguments are compelling and undisputed and that, therefore, they transcend the individual social contexts. In this, he sees the birth of the Natural Law, which treats nature as the foundation of law.

The aspirations of the Natural Law would be frustrated internally, due to the irremediable contrast between different interpretations of what is "natural" and what is not. A typical example is the dispute that arose between the Natural Law about the institution of inheritance, as it was extremely difficult to determine whether the *ordo naturalis* prescribed the return to the community, the transmission from father to son, or the free disposal by the owner[3].

Bobbio emphasizes the elusiveness of the principles of nature, and, therefore, the difficulty of identifying which rights may sink into its roots; past this first hurdle, we would be facing the unresolved question of what is more natural, then having to conclude that this choice depends on the user rather than objective evidence[4].

Kant, according to Bobbio, faced this issue exceptionally, limiting the range of natural rights, concluding that there is only one: freedom.

The Thinker does not share the Kantian perspective and, indeed, notes that even freedom can not be seen as an absolute principle, since there is not one single definition of freedom, and therefore, also ends to represent yet another category relative, subjective, and uncertain.

On the other hand, Bobbio not only questioned the absolute foundation of right, but he goes further: he wonders whether this is desirable, and the answer is resolutely negative.

First, with reference to the history of civilization, there would be no evidence to prove that the existence of an absolute right would be beneficial to individuals. It would not be possible to say that human rights have thrived more in the ages in which the shared opinion of the ruling classes were in favor of the absolute foundation.

Bobbio says that the periods in which the Natural Law has been affirmed represent the moments of maximum harassment of human rights. The Universal Declaration of human rights, in fact, was born in what the philosopher defines the *"period of crisis of foundations."*[5]

Bobbio argues that in the present, the debate about rights should not even be faced as much by philosophy, but rather, by policy, as only in this area can it be guaranteed the affirmation of the principles that have already been sanctioned, and which, therefore, mental speculation would be superfluous for practical purposes.

The best hope would be to seek, not actually an absolute foundation, but, from time to time, the various possible foundations of rights, through complementary tools to philosophy, such as the study of history, society, economics, psychology, etc.[6]

About all those expectations or demands that the philosopher finds in contemporary society and for the inclusion of new forms of protection, he states that:

> I have no objection to call rights also these requests of future rights, as long as you avoid the confusion between a well-reasoned request future protection of a certain good with the effective protection of this good I can get by resorting to a court of justice able to remedy the wrong and possibly punish the guilty. To who does not want to renounce the use of the word right for the demands of future protection motivated on the nature, I would suggest to distinguish between a right in a weak sense and a right in the strong sense, when you do not want to attribute the word right only to requests or demands effectively protected. [7]

Criticism against the Search for an Absolute Foundation of Right

Bobbio is highly critical of a hypothetical absolute foundation of right, and this not only with reference to the idea and its consequences, but even with regard to the research itself, considered liable—as we have seen before—to distract from the substance of the regulatory issues and social issues.

The same existence of the declaration of universal human rights, according to Bobbio, would be enough to frustrate the search for the foundation, or, at least, to make it secondary and negligible compared with the prevailing effort to implement these principles.

Before even starting a logical and philosophical path, it needs to ask the purpose and, if necessary, the utility. According to Bobbio, the search for the absolute foundation of rights would face four problems:

1. the vagueness of the definition;
2. the changing nature of rights in the course of history;
3. the heterogeneity of rights;
4. the antinomy among the rights invoked by the same subjects.

According to his four critical topics, Bobbio concludes that the absolute foundation of right is an illusion, made possible only by the use of preconceived ideas that, to the test of facts and history, would have been for the most tautological and, therefore, self-referential.

If, however, the comparison among these ideas, rights, and actual society is accepted, then the contradictory nature should be noted of the assumptions and the inapplicability of the consequences.

After the failure in finding any absolute foundation, and, indeed, the same concept that lies at its base, we need to rethink the conditions of entitlement, in search of possible referents.

Human Society as Fundament of Right

Bobbio argues that the 1948's Universal Declaration of human rights is sufficient to overcome the issues of interpretation that arose about the foundation
of right. The *consensus omnium gentium*, in fact, represents the only suitable
instrument for the creation of rights and maintaining them; the concept of
universality of natural law is overcome by the principle that considers a law
universal, as it is intended for all mankind.

The assertion of rights under the social consensus would be both universal and positive, since it would lead to a process of creation not limited to
simple formal recognition, but inclusive of the instruments of protection,
including protection against any interference by the State.

The human civilization, not nature, would be the basis of the production
of right, which would pass through three distinct phases: firstly, the rights of
freedom of the individual from the State, then political rights, and, ultimately, social rights.

The third phase, according to Bobbio, would have just started with the
Universal Declaration of human rights, which recognizes new needs and
values, making each State guarantor.

According to Bobbio, the Natural Law would not have allowed a production of comparable rights to those laid down in 1948, as the only "natural"
reaction against violations committed by the State would have consisted in
the resistance.

Social rights have also allowed the widespread recognition of needs on
the basis of distinct groups such as the elders, children, the sick, etc.

To the purposive interpretation of human evolution, typical of the Natural
Law, Bobbio opposes an indeterministic vision, which distances itself from
the so-called *philosophy of history*.

The philosophy of history sees the human evolution as a single process
which, although distinctive in several stages, starts from an origin and turns
toward a particular end; such a procedure, which Kant called "*prophetic
history*," cannot have a cognitive function, but merely suggestive.

Bobbio takes the distance from the Kantian question, whether the human
race is progressing toward the better; in fact, he also argues that the definition
of what is "better" is complex and, ultimately, subjective and imponderable.

In particular, it would be impossible to identify indices suitable for the
measurement of the so-called moral progress of a nation, because the very
concept of morality is problematic and not absolute.

Reflecting on the historical evolution of right, as well as allowing the
exclusion of the teleology of history, according to Bobbio, would help one to
understand the real source, excluding the existence of the absolute law of
nature once and for all.

Men first felt the need for rights in prehistoric times, when they were in a hostile environment, struggling for their very survival, forced to defend themselves not only from other animals, but also from their own kind.

From the basic needs of survival and coexistence the first precepts of morality should be derived, and, consequently, those of law; the example of the Ten Commandments shows that the first rules were mandatory, consisting of commands (do) or prohibitions (do not do).

In Bobbio's opinion, the analysis of the history of law shows that there is a substantial and instantly recognizable difference between animals and humans. Only the latter, in fact, would be motivated by inclinations "*toward the good, or at least toward the correction, limitation, exceeding the evil, which are an essential feature of the human world from the animal world.*"[8]

In Bobbio's view, the *culture* of the man is opposed to the *nature* of the animal, and we can find the precepts of morality only in the first.

Bobbio emphasizes the distinction between animal and human societies is accentuated through the statements of philosophers as Lucretius, Cicero, Hobbes, and Locke, who attributed feral primordial characteristics to men (*homo homini lupus*).

Locke clarifies the main prerogative of the feral condition, which Natural Law assigns to each individual, prior to the adoption of mandatory standards: a status of absolute freedom, limited only by the law of nature[9].

On the other hand, if the rights of the individual come from individualism borrowed from the Natural Law, it is necessary to abandon the ideal of equality in order to establish social rights, typical of the *lex naturalis* (and, in the first place, the authoritative interpretation of it provided by Locke).

Human society (or civilization) would have unequivocally renounced affirmation of the principle of freedom expressed by the individualistic Natural Law, recognizing, however, social solidarity as a value of legislative inspiration.

The Fundament of Nonhuman Rights according to Bobbio

In the definition of right, Bobbio distinguishes between weak rights, characterized by the absence of sanctions, and strong rights, the non-compliance of which implies sanctions[10].

One of the indices of relativism of the right would be its constant evolution/transformation, a process that, according to Bobbio, moves mainly toward the universalization and multiplication.

Bobbio states that there are three main directions in the propagation of rights: first, the increase in assets worthy of protection, then the extension of the ownership of some typical rights to nonhuman entities, and, finally, the consideration of a man in his specificity and social belonging.

Bobbio includes animal and environmental rights in the second category, noting the recurrence of terms such as *"respect"* and *"exploitation,"* exactly as in human rights[11].

The concept of animal rights, devoid of ideological assumptions, is similar to that of any other right—it would change nothing if those rights pertain to persons or other entities, and one should only wonder how these rights can be formed into positive affirmation.

Denying any absolute foundation of right and, at the same time, considering inapplicable the principles of the philosophy of history, Bobbio concludes that animal rights, new rights as others, have been (and will be) recognized in the measure in which they become socially shared.

The refusal of historical teleology also follows the impossibility of drawing certain predictions about the nature and extent of the rights that can be recognized in the future; Bobbio, in fact, argues that the only certainty is that it is impossible for the contemporary observer to predict all those rights that will be developed in the future, as the result of social transformations.

In Bobbio's words:

> The very fact that the list of these rights is constantly increasing not only shows that the starting point of the hypothetical state of nature has lost all plausibility, but also that the world of social relationships from whom these requests derive is highly complex, and so-called fundamental rights, such as life, liberty and property are not enough for life and human survival in this new society.[12]

The most relevant aspect of Bobbio's philosophy about animal rights consists in the total neutrality; in fact, he does not challenge or support such a claim, since he simply does not enter into the merits of the matter.

Other supporters of the contract theory (Rawls in particular) considered the issue of human rights in a much more deterministic way, based on an analysis guided by moral aspects of the rights process elaboration. From this perspective, the "typical" conclusion is to exclude nonhumans from the ownership of any rights.

Searching for a social foundation in the claim for animal rights, Bobbio tries to classify them as *indirect rights*; in fact, the foundation, as well as the revocation, descend exclusively from human will, and it would not even be possible to exclude the possibility that social change could lead to the future repeal of nonhuman rights that had been previously assigned.

According to Bobbio:

> 'right' is a deontic figure, and therefore is a term of legal jargon, a language in which we talk about rules and regulations. The existence of a right, both in the strong sense and in the weak sense, always implies the existence of a regulatory system, where 'existence' can be intended as the mere fact of a historical

right or external force, as the recognition of a set of rules to guide of actions. The figure of right has as correlative the figure of obligation. [13]

Which space may the claims for animal rights have been based on morals? Bobbio answers that moral obligations, like natural ones, cannot have any absolute sense, but they can only have a sense within a legal framework, assuming an objective recognition and a shared sense (the so-called "common sense").

Nor would it be correct to speak of *"moral rights,"* given the specificity of the term "right": those instances would be needs that may rise to the level of rights, if they have been implemented by positive law.

A typical example of the difference between an instance or a claim and the actual existence of a right is the case of conscientious objection. It would be impossible to speak of a *"right to conscientious objection"* in a nation that had not recognized such a legal institute. In this, as in other similar cases, there would only be a weak right, and, possibly, the affirmation of an obligation, asking to recognize it under the law.

It seems consistent with the above, also serving as a warning to ensure better enforcement of rights, rather than continually extending the debate on their origin.

Bobbio has expressed interest in the evolution of the rights, intended to also encompass those of animals, stating:

> Never before as in our era have the three main sources of inequality been challenged: class, race, and sex. The gradual equalization of women to men, first in small family society and then in the largest civil and political society, is one of the surest signs of the unstoppable journey of mankind toward equality. And what about the new attitude towards animals? Debates become more frequent and extended, concerning the legality of the hunt, the limits of vivisection, the protection of animal species become increasingly rare, vegetarianism, what are if not signs of a possible extension of the principle of equality, even beyond the boundaries of the human race, an extension based on the awareness that animals are equal to us men, at least in the ability to suffer? We understand that to grasp the meaning of this great historical movement one should raise his head from the daily skirmishes and look higher and farther. [14]

The abovesaid considerations seem perfectly in line with Bobbio's thought about any rethinking of the rights and the refusal to consider them as limited or defined.

Michael Ignatieff and the Foundation of Law in the Consensus among States

The Canadian philosopher Michael Ignatieff shares Bobbio's perspective about the foundation of right, deeming the universalism of Natural Law theories inadmissible and considering the right founded on the consent of the historical and social context that produced it.

Ignatieff does not just criticize the doctrine of Natural Law, but also distances himself from Ethical Relativism, accused of rendering impossible the formation of a certain set of rules whose application can be considered reasonably established and indispensable.

The Canadian philosopher warns against the danger of the instrumental use of rights, which he illustrates with the metaphor of "trumps," arguing that

> Human rights could take a less imperial character if they became more politi-cal, or if they were not perceived as a language issue and proclaim the eternal truths, but as a speech for the solution of conflicts. [...] If the rights and conflicted requests cannot be arranged in accordance with unquestionable mo-ral priority, it is not possible to consider the rights as trumps. [...] At best, the rights create a common framework, in shared set of reference points that can be of assistance to the parties in conflict to dialogue.[15]

The main risk of the rights universalism would be to create a sort of new religion, aimed toward affirming absolute principles from ideas that, by defi-nition, cannot be absolute.

Ignatieff takes into consideration, outside of the individual communities, the international level, where the assumption of supranational juridical relati-vism shows its limits; in fact, since the fundament of right is in social con-sensus, it is clear that such consent, strongly affected by the context of origin, tend to fade out of it, thus losing its validity.

Ignatieff concludes that the foundation of human rights lies in the consen-sus among countries, and that it is possible to escape both from ethical relativism and universalism of Natural Law through the identification of a small group of internationally agreed rights, on the recognition of which each country agrees.

Ignatieff's reflections flow into the so-called *Minimalist Universalism.* It would be possible to say that certain legal principles have absolute value, but only under certain conditions.

First, the category of absolute principles must be restricted out of neces-sity; even their foundation cannot be considered abstract or transcendent, but, on the contrary, must be rooted in the will and perception of the community, intended as a community of nations.

Like any common denominator, even those relating to human rights, ac-cording to Ignatieff, can be determined using a scientific method; it is neces-sary to take into account the rights that each country recognizes as funda-mental or inalienable and place them in comparison with those considered as such by the other countries, discarding those that are not shared.

According to Ignatieff, this core of universal rights can be defined starting from those behaviors that represent the most serious violations against people: genocide, racial discrimination, torture, inhumane treatment, and violation of the principle of self-determination of peoples.

In the universal-minimalist view, there is no place for the so-called "freedoms to," but only for the "freedoms from," that is, negative freedoms that Isaiah Berlin intended as *"the ability of each individual to achieve rational purposes without obstacle or hindrance."* [16]

Ignatieff's idea can be considered as a *"light theory"* of right, intended as a *"mere definition of the minimum conditions for all kinds of life,"* [17] and that definition is opposed to the moral perspective to determine what is "good" rather than "right." The distinction would be necessary to prevent the danger of imperialism colonialism that Ignatieff derives from the moral universalism, which, annihilating pluralism, opens the door to dictatorship.

Ignatieff distinguishes between individual rights and collective rights, no doubt leaning in favor of the former, because he says: *"can be difficult to exercise individual rights without collective rights, but collective rights without individual rights result in the tyranny."* [18]

Ignatieff's work is strongly characterized by pragmatism; in fact, he concludes that policy is the fundamental means to claim rights.

Ignatieff represents a sort of passing of Bobbio's positions, which, although shared in many assumptions, are further developed through innovative solutions.

There is also a parallelism between Ignatieff and Luigi Ferrajoli's definition of fundamental rights as *"all those rights which belong universally to"* all *"human beings since they have the status of persons, or citizens or people who are able to act."* [19]

According to Ferrajoli, the fundamental rights are also universal rights, because they are provided to all human beings without distinction. For this reason, they must also be considered unavailable and inalienable.

Ferrajoli's positivist conception is also reflected in the distinction that he makes between fundamental rights on the basis of citizenship and capacity to contract, intended as parameters to discriminate between *personal rights* and *rights of citizenship*. From these references Ferrajoli identifies four classes of rights, namely human rights, public, civil, and political rights.

A point of contact between Ferrajoli and Ignatieff is in the analysis of the internationalization of fundamental rights, a phenomenon that Ferrajoli considers to be one of the main achievements of the twentieth century. Both authors attribute the effectiveness and the realization of the rights to the internationalization, as opposed to their mere assertion in the group of weak rights.

From the above, Ferrajoli borrows the concept of *universal citizenship*, considering the spread of international organizations and, on the other hand, moving sharply critical to the rules based on sovereign states, unable to

effectively regulate the community, and, conversely, the causes of conflicts.[20]

Ignatieff's link between universalism and relativism shows a pragmatic
imprint, also typical of Ferrajoli, anchored in the contemporary socio-political context, which includes himself, actively engaged in policy, as an actor as
well as an observer.

Ignatieff, unlike Bobbio, goes so far as to suggest what fundamental
rights the States must ensure; his thought also shows the same neutrality
about predictable rights as Bobbio's, and the result seems to be a kind of
hybrid model between Natural Law and Positivism.

From the Natural Law, Ignatieff borrowed the concept of fundamental
rights, while their foundation is attributed to social consensus (mainly in its
international dimension).

Ignatieff does not mention animal rights, nor does it seem possible to
recognize them in his theory, given the exclusively human nature of fundamental rights that he considers worthy of protection.

Ignatieff's theory of right might suggest that nothing prohibits the introduction of rules for the protection of beings different from humans into
national law, but that does not in any way alter the *numerus clausus* of
fundamental rights recognized by the international consensus.

Attilio Pisanò and Dehumanized Rights

Pisanò, jurist and philosopher of law, starting from Bobbio's premises, analyzed the implications underlying the multiplication of right-holders.

According to Pisanò, the fact that, for the first time in history, rights are
being accorded to nonhuman subjects, poses certain problems.

> Both philosophical and legal, as we are, as mentioned facing a new way (often
> rhetorical) to understand the semantic meaning, the role, the function of rights.
> The terms animal rights, environmental rights, rights of future generations, the
> rights of the human species break the classic, modern, and contemporary, that
> sees individual rights be specified through reference to man.[21]

Pisanò contrasts, not without criticism, the new perspectives of the right
to the Cartesian traditional formulation. The perspective of the human subject as the conceptual center of the Right, he said, is now under review,
especially from animal rights activists and environmentalists, who claim the
ownership of legal positions against different bodies by man.[22] The scope of
the discussion is what Bobbio called *"weak rights."* These are, by definition,
all those rights that Pisanò considers as instances for the future recognition of
expectations, outside the context of individual human rights.

Pisanò uses the term *dehumanization* to allude to the *"classical sense of
the ignorance of the human qualities against individuals degraded to objects,*

but in the sense, again, paradigmatic, revolutionary, controversial, which attributes to objects [...] values, appearance, expectations, interests modeled on human subjectivity."[23]

Pisanò argues that the process of dehumanization of Right is currently confined to philosophy rather than to positive law—in the latter there has not yet been any transposition of matter.

The change in course would result from the denial of the privileged human status over everything else (animals, environment, etc.). One of the side effects would consist in the inflation of the term *Right*, and in the above-mentioned generic that it would adopt in the changed context.

Of course, once a Pandora's box of rights is uncovered, it will be quickly followed by a search for an answer to the question: "What beings will have citizenship in the group of new legal entities?" The answer to this question presupposes the ability of finding a criterion to serve as a distinction between the different categories, which, according to Pisanò, will be a difficult task and far from uncontroversial.

Despite the risks resulting from the introduction of new categories of rights, Pisanò considers the comparison as necessary and pressing, both for law and for philosophy, since they are responsible for determining the criteria and methods of change and extension of the concept of right.

Pisanò suggests another critical issue: in the age of human rights, pressures towards dehumanization often take on a connotation opposite to that anthropocentric, with the result to determine a kind of antinomy hard to solve.

If, in fact, it is true that the modern age has given birth to the idea of animal and environmental rights, it is true that, in Positive Law, the predominance for the establishment, expansion, and specification of human rights have prevailed.

Is it therefore possible to reconcile the *Universal Declaration of Human Rights* with the principle of dehumanization? According to Pisanò, it is, because the main underlying philosophical statement to both events is non-discrimination, which some limit to mankind and others extend to nonhuman contexts.

Pisanò proves his thesis through the etymology of the term "speciesism," which was coined by psychologist RD Ryder in 1975[24] from the concepts of racism and sexism.[25] In this sense, the origin of speciesism is radicated in an anthropocentric perspective, or, at least, in the wake of principles widely used for the definition of purely human social behavior.[26]

Another clue to the cultural proximity between human rights and dehumanized rights would be recognized by the fact that the latter has found its greatest expression in Western societies, though the eastern ones are far more distant from the anthropocentric principle of European-Christian matrix.

Finally, Pisanò argues, it is clear that the Universal Declaration of Animal Rights (1978), the Universal Declaration of Human rights of Future Generations (1994), and the Universal Declaration of Rights of Mother Earth (2010) are confined in the wake of the Universal Declaration of Human Rights, drawing much more than a simple inspiration; in particular, there would not be only commonality of principles between these statements, but also of tools:

1. use the language of rights;
2. use of the term "Declaration";
3. reference to universality that does not represent the facts, but of which it is hoped the recognition.

The final question proposed by the author regards the possibility of considering the expansion of subjects of Law as an advancement of legal science and society. To define the matter is, however, necessary to provide a preliminary definition of the term *progress*. What can be called progress? What, also, is regression?

According to Pisanò we need to discern between purely legal, on one hand, and moral implications on the other hand, underlying the concept of progress.

> Of course, the extension of the principles of justice and equality among species is certainly different from the human moral progress. But, legally speaking, the issues raised today by animal rights, the rights of great apes, the rights of nature, the biosphere, biotic community, represent a step forward in the history of individual rights or, rather, bear witness to a regression, a return to positions pregrotians, prehumanistic?[27]

Pisanò recommends maintaining, firm and unshakable, Grotius's definition of right, of humanistic matrix and considered essential in the process of extending the concept to entities other than man.[28]

The solution to ensure both moral and legal progress, according to Pisanò, would be in adopting a different terminology, which abandons the concept of right in the technical sense of Grotius memory, rather evolving toward different models for both definitions and concepts.

So Pisanò argues not a rejection of the anthropocentric conception of right, but its consolidation, as well as exploring new places, from which to draw for dehumanized categories.[29]

Pisanò's view reflects a deep and analytical evaluation of legal aspects that underlie moral thought; he consistently supports the pragmatism of Positive Law, considering it an essential reference and natural corollary of all the philosophies of law.

Pisanò's thought seems to be a perfect bridge between the more strongly anthropocentric perspectives, opposite to the dehumanization of rights and the other that, instead, criticizes anthropocentrism, accepting some of Bobbio's precepts, and agreeing that the law can be extended to nonhuman entities.

If Pisanò's theory about the primary role of human rights seems to embrace the anthropocentric theories of the law, the same cannot be said about the theories of the animal rights philosophers, who claim the application of the conceptual category of right also for nonhumans.

1.2 PETER SINGER AND ANIMALS IN THE UTILITARIAN PERSPECTIVE

Jeremy Bentham and the Foundation of Utilitarianism

Even before starting to talk about animal rights, or at least of those that Bobbio called *weak rights* or *expectations*, the Western philosophy began to take its first steps toward nonhuman subjects, particularly of animals, with Bentham and Utilitarianism.

In 1780 the publication of Jeremy Bentham's *Introduction to the Principles of Morals and Legislation* marked the foundation of Utilitarianism.

In that work, eminently dedicated to the right, Bentham sets out his belief that morality can be expressed by using an algebraic formula; the morality of an action would be directly proportional to the well-being made by it, and therefore, as already theorized by Hume, apart from abstract considerations and from the absolute principle that inspired the theory of natural law.

According to Bentham, happiness should be intended as the realization of fulfillment in conjunction with the absence of suffering; his idea of morality is entirely inspired by this fundamental perspective.

The detachment from the Natural Law is evident: while the first implies the existence of absolute precepts, to be respected irrespective of the implications, utilitarianism refuses the same idea of absolute rules, instead considering the point of view of the result.

The foundations of Bentham's moral philosophy essentially lies on three characteristics that he considers and examines in all his works:

- the principle of maximum happiness (or utility principle);
- universal selfishness;
- identification of a fictitious interest with that of others.

The pursuit of the greatest happiness of each would coincide, according to Bentham, with that of all the others. First, in fact, when you claim that the pursuit of happiness represents an absolute good, then it would not be pos-

sible to discriminate between your own happiness and that of others, believing that only the first is a good thing.

While taking note of the human tendency to selfishness, Bentham believes that this does not affect acting in accordance with morality, since even
the selfish actions would be spontaneously oriented to the principle of utility
and, therefore, though unintentionally, morally oriented.

In light of the above, Bentham concludes that the interests of one should
be identified with those of all the others and, as such, seconded and taken
into account in accordance with the principle of equal value of each, expressed in the statement: "*each person is to count for one and no one for
more than one.*"[30]

An explanation of utilitarianism provided by Bentham himself describes
the theory of morality as "*the art of directing men's actions to the production
of the greatest possible quantity of happiness, on the part of those whose
interest is in view.*"[31]

Bentham's thought appears to be the first formulation of a modern moral
theory that takes into account nonhuman animals.

Since Utilitarianism, as stated, refers to the happiness of a group of individuals in order to determine the morality of actions; one of the preliminary
issues is the definition of the target group—the happiness of which individuals *deserve* consideration? Answering this question, Bentham recognizes the
moral status of nonhuman animals, stating that: "*The question is not 'Can
they reason?' nor 'Can they talk?' but 'Can they suffer?'*"[32] By this statement, Bentham changes the philosophical conception of nonhuman animals.
Many had debated whether they had the ability to think or not, or if they had
a soul, but the father of Utilitarianism has radically shifted the discriminant,
considering the right to not suffer as an immediate and exclusive consequence of the attitude to suffer, while noting that the nature or amount of
intellect or the ability of expression should not be taken into consideration.

R.M. Hare and the Two-level Utilitarianism

Utilitarianism has evolved, distinguishing, among others, two opposing
schools of thought, one called *of act* and the other called *of rule*. In the first
an action morally correct is identified as being able to deliver the greater
possible good in practice, while in the second case the moral evaluation is
carried out in relation to the observance of a rule that, if followed by everyone, is deemed to lead to greater prosperity.

Hare's philosophy, or at least that of the second phase of his thought,
synthesizes these two perspectives and is aptly named the *Utilitarianism of
Preferences of Two Levels*. Hare's two levels are the *intuitive* and the *critical*
one.

The first level would be used to act every day, manifested in the choices that each of us is required to perform, which are not based on a real critical analysis or reflection, but are guided by the intuitive perception that each person would have regarding what is right and what is not, based on what causes (or does not cause) damage.

In short, all of us would be aware that a harmful act against others would be morally reprehensible and, therefore, even without special tools or logical critics, we would be prepared to act in accordance with the precepts of Utilitarianism.

The critical level would be the only possible one to determine the correct behavior in unexpected, out of the ordinary situations, and in a systematic and universal way; at this level, according to Hare, the morality should be guided by the Utilitarian thought, in all its implications.

The three basic requirements that Hare attributes to moral judgments are:

- *universalizability*;
- *overridingness*;
- *prescriptivity*.

According to the first requirement, the moral judgment must be valid in all cases that are similar in moral terms, while any subjectification, through which the observer would recognize a higher value to its own interests, should be rejected.

The overridingness implies that, in the event of a conflict between moral norms and rules otherwise, the first should prevail.

Prescriptivity, which is also considered the most controversial requirement, implies that one sincerely assents to a moral judgment only acting consistently with it, wherever it applies, at least while other things are equal.

From the last prerogative also comes the definition of Hare's thought as *Universal Prescriptivism*; this theory implies that moral judgments should be applicable to all cases similar to the original ones, prevailing over any other motivation. In this way, he separates logic and judgment from any interest of the observer, stating that all the expectations, perceptions, advantages, and damage must be considered in accordance to the individual and not abstractly.

According to Hare, *empathy* is the fundamental tool to perform all of the above—only by immersing yourself in others, beneficiaries of actions, is it possible to correctly evaluate the interests at stake and, therefore, act in accordance with Utilitarianism's requirements.

Gary Varner derives his theory from Hare's two-level theory, making it his own, and arguing about the relationship between human and nonhuman animals.

Varner uses empirical data and scientific studies to understand the nature of animals and, consequently, reflects on their moral attributions. From these observations, he concludes that there would be several different categories to consider, since it is not possible to only distinguish between humans and nonhumans.

More precisely, Varner argues the existence of three categories:

* *persons*;
* *near-persons*;
* *merely sentient beings.* [33]

The first status belongs only to humans, who, he argues, are characterized by exclusive prerogatives such as the ability to tell stories, to have a sense of the development of life and, therefore, to draw in this regard presumptions and expectations. [34]

If, on the one hand, the status of persons is limited to humans, Varner argues that, on the other hand, certain animal species should be considered similar, and, therefore, *almost persons*—in such rank would be included primates, dolphins, and rats, as well as, probably, elephants, whales, and crows. [35]

By combining his observations with Hare's two-level Utilitarianism, Varner concludes that the first level, that is intuitive, should incorporate the principle of not killing sentient animals unnecessarily. [36]

Varner's formulation does not discuss the merits of the principle of necessity, renouncing providing any conclusions about the method to distinguish between the justified and those that, lacking the requirement of necessity, instead, would be unjustified.

Hare's theory involves the replaceability of individuals and, therefore, both human and nonhuman would be replaceable; the death of some could be compensated for, in a global sense, through the creation of new beings with expectations that will be fulfilled. [37]

Varner argues that eating meat, according to the principle of replaceability, would not be wrong in an absolute way, but, as Hare stated, it should be done by ensuring:

* the maximization of the welfare of animals;
* the replacement of individuals killed with others;
* the limitation of consumption.

The application of the three precepts, according to Varner, should make farming sustainable and make it possible to include animals in the evaluation of preferences (and thus welfare), taking them into account in the context of moral judgment.

In Varner's view, a limitation of consumption would be needed to allow the use of extensive rather than intensive farming and, therefore, would be functional to the need of maximizing the welfare of farming animals. Once the conditions of life in farms have reached a standard so high as to make the existence of the animal pleasant until the time of slaughter, it would be possible to apply the principle of subrogation and, therefore, the level of global well-being would be higher than the damage inflicted by killing, by ensuring that the number of individuals disposed of corresponds to the creation of the same number of substitutes that can live a pleasant life.

Peter Singer and the Preference Utilitarianism

Peter Singer, one of Hare's former students, was inspired by his Preference Utilitarianism and he joined Utilitarianism.

Acting in an ethical manner, in Singer's view, means to give importance to all the preferences of the individuals taken into account, or in any way involved in the consequences of a decision.

Individuals whose preferences are to be relevant, according to Singer, however, would not only be humans, but also nonhuman animals.

In 1975, Singer wrote *Animal Liberation*, reflecting on the human-animal relationship in the contemporary world, to prove that the suffering and exploitation caused by humans to nonhumans are wrongful. In particular, an entire chapter of the book was dedicated to vegetarianism, which he defines as a moral obligation.

> The first step is to stop eating animals. Many people who oppose animal cruelty, stop at the prospect of becoming vegetarian. About such persons, Oliver Goldsmith, the humanitarian thinker of the eighteenth century, writes: 'They feel pity and eat the objects of their compassion '[...] Becoming vegetarian is the most practical and effective step that you can take to put an end to so much infliction of suffering to nonhuman animals as to killing them. [38]

Singer's thought is an evolution of Bentham's Utilitarianism, and this is evident in the considerations of the first about vegetarianism: *"If we are willing to take the life of another being only in order to satisfy our taste for a particular kind of food, that being is nothing more than a means to our ends. [...] Factory farming is nothing more than the application of technology to the idea that animals are a means to our ends."* [39]

Just as Bentham before him, Singer focuses on the concept of suffering, arguing: *"How can anyone who has examined in depth the issue know that the problem of animal suffering is less serious than that of human suffering? You can expect to know only if it is assumed that animals don't really count and that, regardless of how they suffer, their suffering is less important than that of humans."* [40]

The moral system proposed by Singer, which extends well beyond the consideration of nonhuman animals, rests primarily on what he calls *New Commandments*, that is five precepts in opposition to the traditional commandments of the Christian Religion:

1. *Recognize that the worth of human life varies;*
2. *Take responsibility for the consequences of our decisions;*
3. *Respect a person's desire to live or die;*
4. *Bring children into the world only if they are wanted;*
5. *Do not discriminate on the basis of species.* [41]

The rejection of discrimination arises from the consideration, characteristic of Singer's view, that not all humans would be persons in the moral sense of the term and not all nonhuman animals [42] would be non-persons.

The moral person, who is capable of understanding the implications of actions and distinguishing them on the basis of making choices, could not be identified with humans suffering from severe mental impairments or with children, while at least some animals would be capable of that.

Singer's definition of a person is similar to that of Hugo Tristram Engelhardt, Jr., according to whom it is not possible to define all men as persons, but only those who possess certain qualities or characteristics: self-consciousness, rationality, a minimum sense of morality and freedom. [43]

At the antipodes of Singer, Robert Spaemann argues that all human beings, including those severely disabled, must possess the status of person, identifying all members of the human species [44] with this term.

While not openly declaring that he shared Spaemann's view, Varner criticizes Singer, as he considers viewing animals at the status of persons unsustainable; Varner claims that such arguments aren't convincing and, therefore, he suggests that Singer should take into account the category of so-called *near-persons*, rather than artificially attributing the same condition of human beings to certain animals.

On the other hand, Varner emphasizes that the hypothetical downgrade would not hinder the assertion of moral obligations toward animals considered *near-persons.* [45]

Varner's statement seems convincing, at least in pointing out that the equivalence between moral statuses is not necessary to include heterogeneous categories in a moral system. One could definitely say that the fact that different individuals have different levels of moral attributions does not imply result in automatic exclusion of a category on a hierarchical basis.

The Principle of Equal Consideration of Interests

Singer himself indicated the *Equal Consideration of Interests* as his cardinal principle, which refers to the well-known Bentham's precept: "*Each person is to count for one and no one for more than one.*"[46]

Just as Bentham had, Singer also concluded that there would be no reason to exclude nonhuman animals from the consideration of the interests intended to determine the morality of an action.

Singer argues that there would not be any difference between denying nonhuman animals' interests the same consideration of the humans' and discriminating among humans on the basis of race, gender, or other personal characteristics: speciesism would be only a particular form of discrimination based on prejudice and, as such, despicable and morally unjustified.

Since you cannot understand the suffering of others, nor measure it, according to Singer, you could not even say that humans have the right to dispose of nonhumans while causing them pain, as by doing so you would commit an arbitrary act; Singer, in fact, believes that "*the limit of sensitivity is the only defensible boundary to take into account the interests of others. Drawing this boundary by other characteristics, such as intelligence or rationality, would be arbitrary.*"[47]

Singer also considers the key parameter of his own moral attitude to be that of the ability of a being to experience pain and suffering. He argues that: "*If a being suffers, there can be no moral justification for refusing to take that suffering into consideration.*"[48]

Singer does not deny differences between human and nonhuman animals, and, in particular, he recognizes their *self-consciousness*, as the perception of the flowing of time and the maturation of expectations for the future—that skill, typical of human beings, would expose them to more suffering.

According to the classical theories of Utilitarianism, death would result in damage only to those who can mature expectations toward the future, while it would not be considered an absolute evil in and of itself, nor could it be for people who lack the ability to represent the future and have expectations connected.

It would be justifiable killing animals that, lacking aspirations about their future existence, would not suffer damage in the utilitarian sense of the term.

To the abovementioned objections, Singer argues that the inability of nonhuman animals to represent the future might imply less anxiety on the one hand, but, on the other hand, it could determine the exact opposite. To explain his assertion, he makes the example of the animals used in cosmetics or pharmacological testing, experiencing the deprivation of liberty in the first place, but that, unlike humans, could not appeal to the consolation felt from the presumption of a return to freedom.

In analyzing the implications of the mental faculties and self-understanding by human and nonhuman animals, Singer proposes a topic that many found provocative or even offensive; in fact, he makes humans suffering from mental disabilities equal to animals, stating that if you intend to justify the exploitation of the latter because of their lower intellectual abilities, the same should be allowed for human persons with disabilities.

From the principle of equal consideration of interests, Singer argues that the food issue is a fundamental problem of daily moral acting.

In this case, according to Singer's view, the interests involved have completely different ranks; on the one hand, the sensory satisfaction of the human beings and, on the other hand, the animals' need to not suffer and to exist.

If a human population (Singer refers to Eskimos) need to eat animals to survive, according to Singer, this could be seen as a moral justification for such action, while outside of this hypothesis, in civilized societies, it would be a foregone conclusion that the infliction of suffering and death to animals for food, representing something unnecessary, cannot find any justification.

Moreover, the death and suffering, in Singer's Utilitarianism view, are two concepts clearly distinguished that cannot be confused; indeed, he shares the utilitarian perspective that prevents us from considering death as an absolute evil, arguing that this would be true only in case of frustration of aspirations and expectations.

On the contrary, a death that would prevent suffering—particularly euthanasia—can be considered a positive even in the utilitarian sense of the term. This is the conclusion of the Australian philosopher, and, therefore, he contests the use of intensive farming for food in the first place.

In farming, Singer argues, all animals are forced to live in unnatural conditions, and this in itself implies a suffering that is compounded significantly by the methods applied.

The philosopher justifies his position by stating that this is due to the fact that the second half of the 900 conventional breeding of animals has been gradually replaced by a more specialized form, which, making use of science and technology, has sought to maximize profits by minimizing costs.

Selection and genetic alteration of entire races would determine the occurrence of diseases, impairments, and sufferings of various kinds, and beside it, the spaces of farms decreased and from conditions of outdoor permanence or grazing, we moved to detention indoors, force-feeding, artificial night/day cycles, and the use of cages of smaller dimensions.

Even the natural feeding of farmed animals has been transformed by the use of cheaper food that accelerates growth, though at the expense of the health and welfare of individuals.

For all the above, Singer concludes that the suffering of an animal bred through the intensive method is far superior to that of an animal that, for example, lived its whole life in freedom and nature and is killed by a hunting human being.

The Australian philosopher emphasizes the contradictory and unfounded moral position of the majority of people, who claim to be opposed to hunting but do not practice vegetarianism. Due to the outstanding amount of suffering inflicted by the breeding and the much more modest amount connected with hunting, the morally oriented conclusion should be the exact opposite.

About hunting, Singer expresses a firm conviction, recognizing in particular:

- Lack of need;
- Suffering of hunted animals;
- Non-substitutability.

Similar to farming, even in the case of hunting, it would not be possible to find any moral justification, as there is no need.

Nor would it be acceptable to conduct hunts for the purpose of maintenance of habitats or environmental resources. Since one would be able to achieve this end through sterilization, utilitarianism would require one to choose the latter as an alternative solution that maximizes the importance of the interests of those involved (also of animals), minimizing the suffering of all.

Singer also notes that in the case of hunting it would not even be possible to recognize the existence of the principle of replaceability. If, on the one hand, the amount of suffering inflicted on animals in factory farming is crucial and leads to the rejection of such a practice from the utilitarian perspective, on the other side, the replacement of individuals in such a system is constant.

When a hunter suppresses, for example, a duck, there isn't any replacement by the birth of another individual, whose fulfilled expectations can compensate for the loss of those of the one killed.

It would be incorrect to think that Singer put the interests of animals before those of human beings. He did, however, confirm the full application of Utilitarianism in also taking a position on the experiments conducted for medical and scientific.

If the proposed experiments were necessary to safeguard the interest in the lives of men, Singer says, it would be possible to justify the sacrifice of an animal, compensating for the loss with the advantage of protecting the lives of many human individuals. In this case, Singer insists that we must attribute greater importance to the life of a being endowed with self-awareness and a perception of time, compared to that of a being without these attributes.

On the other hand, Singer clarifies that the above speculation is purely academic, since the usefulness of the experiments is uncertain and that, as mentioned, based on the utilitarian principle, the same justification of animal tests would also allow experiments on mentally disabled humans.

Utilitarianism does not imply that everyone should be treated in the same way, but, as Singer argues: *"The fundamental principle of equality does not require equal or identical treatment. It prescribes equal consideration; an equal consideration for different beings may lead to a different treatment and different rights."*[49]

Critical to Naturalism and Contractualism

Singer faced various aspects of Natural Law that are frequently used to deny animal rights, and, in particular, with regard to vegetarianism: it would, in fact, be "natural" feeding off other animals as this is normally done even outside of human society.

The Australian philosopher argues that human beings don't usually borrow their behaviors from those of nonhuman and that, moreover, carnivores have no choice, so this would be a necessity and not mere wishful thinking.

The instinct, which, according to Singer, would be dominant in the case of animals, would cause each to feed according to its predisposition; in the case of humans, however, there would be no instinct to bite into a living animal. Based on these arguments, Singer rejects any moral justification of meat consumption based on the so-called "laws of nature" and, indeed, opposes the instinctual action typical of nonhuman animals to the moral that distinguishes the people, determining responsibility at the same time.

In conceptual terms, Singer denies the possibility to credit actions to unidentified principles of nature, and he argues that these considerations have been the basis of racism, sexism, classism, etc.

Singer also refuses Contractualism, and, in particular, he opposes the consideration that animals could not enjoy rights because they are unable to assume duties toward us and, therefore, to participate in the so-called *Social Contract* that would be the basis of right.

Even in this case, the Australian philosopher insists that the same exclusion of animals from the list of possible contractors should cover all the immature humans (children) or mentally disabled, since they are unable to assume duties or understand the fundamentals of the social contract.

Eating and Morals

Singer's Utilitarianism applied in human-animal relationships led the author to recognize relevant behavioral inconsistencies in Western civilization; he says that the food issue is fundamental and cannot reasonably be limited to those, secondary in his opinion, who animate many animal rights movements.

Singer compares the number of animals used in vivisection laboratories in the United States (between twenty and forty million) to the number of animals slaughtered, stating that the consumption of meat causes the same amount of deaths in just two days. [50]

Considering the apparent discrepancy between the intention that many declare, to reduce animal suffering, and the increasing consumption of meat, Singer suggests that some mental or cultural mechanism causes a kind of schizophrenia—the majority of people, in short, would not be able to understand the moral implications of meat-eating.

Singer attributes at least some of the responsibility of the so-called *moral schizophrenia* to Christian ideas, as ancient pagan cultures emphasized the relationship with food in a much more conscious and responsible view of an inner and environmental balance. [51] In Singer's view, even the main contemporary religions would focus the faithful's attention on the implications of food, but the practical relevance attributed to the latter precept would be marginal compared to other moral norms of religious doctrine.

According to Singer, in short, Christians are not sufficiently called to dwell on the moral implications underlying eating, focusing instead on precepts such as respect for human life ("do not kill") or property ("do not steal").

The correct attribution of the moral implications of eating would also be precluded due to a cultural phenomenon typical of Western societies in recent decades, which has assigned a prominent and essential role to meat. In so doing, meat has become indispensable for many, and especially to overcome any moral objections, or even prevent them.

The industrialization of farming has distanced consumers from the actual perception of the food chain and, therefore, from the understanding of the underlying pains involved.

Given the importance of wellness (and its opposite, illness) on Utilitarianism's perspective, it is clear that the moral judgment appears distorted when people are unable to imagine the consequences of their choices, namely the amount of suffering inflicted.

According to Singer, the meat producers would have systematically pursued an obscurantist policy, since the public awareness of sufferings inflicted would damage the market, causing a decrease in consumption.

Singer's moral formulation leads to the conclusion of a need to not only censure intensive farming, but also extensive or organic farming, which many consumers consider ethical, and, for such reason, choose the meat from animals raised outdoors.

The arguments in favor of the consumption of these products are as follows:

- *the domestication would be a mutual benefit, the result of evolution;*
- *the animals in this condition would be happy;*
- *death does not imply distress (and thus suffering).* [52]

The first argument is rejected on the grounds that it's impossible to attribute an expression of will or a finality to an entire species that, in reality, can only be expressed individually.

The fact that the number of domesticated animals is significantly higher than those in the wild would not prove any advantage to the first, considered from the point of view of each individual.

About the second argument, Singer argues that there would be no certainty about the happiness of the animals bred with this non-intensive method—that, in fact, does not prevent them from being held in cages or in overcrowded spaces.

The transportation from the place of farming to the place of slaughter would be a further cause of trauma, exacting more distress and suffering that cannot be eliminated.

As for the methods of transport and killing, then, there would be no difference between intensive and extensive animal farming, leaving no alternate conclusion from the fact that—at least at this stage—the suffering and deprivation are entirely analogous.

Singer concludes that, as long as the competition and the pursuit of maximum profit will push farmers to the production of meat, it will be impossible to eliminate the suffering—even the useless occurrences—of the animals.

From the above, it also follows the objection to the third argument, since, when they are killed, there would be no distinction between animals raised free from those caged.

Singer argues that there would be a marked difference in moral terms between those who practice vegetarianism and those who, instead, claim to accept only meat provided by non-intensive farming, at least since the second category of individuals have not met certain lines of demarcation, and in any case, one would externalize the moral persuasion that eating animals is correct. Vegetarians and vegans, clearly and systematically refusing whole categories of products, would be able to steer the market, causing significant transformations of the economic production.

Singer's work has led to the development of the modern animal rights movement, inspired by the publication of his *Animal Liberation*, and is still at the center of the debate about animal rights, as demonstrated by the recent critical work of Varner.

Of course, there are also complaints against Singer's thought process, including accusations of extremism as well as conservatism. On the one hand, the comparison of certain animals to humans and his statements on abortion and the value of life represented a strong position against more established moral values in Western society; on the other hand, the most passionate animal rights advocates sustain that Singer lacks the main conceptual tools necessary to ensure the affirmation of real rights.

Apart from the considerations, more or less critical, toward the effectiveness of Singer's contribution to the cause of animal rights, it cannot be denied that the philosophical system that he developed has few equals, particularly because it is not limited to the animal question, but far more comprehensive and widely innovative.

The relationship between Utilitarianism and the moral conception of nonhuman animals is an argument of interest. It was the founder of this philosophy, Jeremy Bentham, who formulated for the first time a complete philosophical theory that also included the interests of nonhumans, while one of the leading contemporary exponents of this current has been (at least partially) the inspiration behind the new animal rights movements. Still others, like Varner, accepting the principles of Utilitarianism or its specific forms, are still giving new impetus to the development of theories that, if it were not to be strictly defined "Animal rights," certainly have the goal (and effect) to elevate the nonhumans to a level where their interests deserve consideration.

1.3 TOM REGAN, BEYOND UTILITARIANISM

Deontologism, Contract Theory, and Theories of Indirect Duties

Utilitarianism is not alone in considering the question of the relationship between humans and nonhumans, although in this philosophy we find the first formulation of the duties toward animals. Deontologism and Contractualism, at least in the expression of some of their exponents, also arrived at conclusions similar in some ways.

One of the main distinctions among the kind of duties highlighted in different philosophical currents is that between *direct* and *indirect duties*.

The fundamental assumption to be considered holders of direct duties is traditionally identified in the ownership of a morally relevant position; those who are able to make choices are undoubtedly considered morally oriented recipients of direct duties, while it is controversial whether this could also be due to those who do not have this option.

According to Kant, who is considered the founder of Deontologism, moral agents, or, as he called them, *reasonable beings*, are those individuals characterized by the principle of autonomy—they are subjects able to determine ideal values of universal value, thereby judging their actions.[53]

According to the second formulation of Kant's Categorical Imperative of morality, all agents must always be treated as ends and never as means, but such formulation excludes nonhuman animals, as they are considered irrational.

Kant distinguishes between *persons* and *things*: the first category belongs to human beings, intended as moral agents, while animals are included in the second category.

Despite person status being denied to animals, Kant's philosophy recognizes the existence of duties toward them, and, in particular, he states that: *"There are no direct duties towards them, but only duties that are indirect duties towards humanity. Because animals possess a similar nature to that of men, observing duties towards them, we observe duties to humanity, thereby promoting the connected duties."*[54]

According to Kant, the manifestation of cruelty to animals would be reprehensible as a symptom of insensitivity toward men: *"Man must show goodness of heart towards animals, since those who use to be cruel to them is just as insensitive toward men."*[55]

Regan criticizes Kant's view about duties to animals, arguing that it betrays a contradiction between the principles expressed by the same Kant; the analogy between cruelty to animals and to humans suggests that both of them feel suffering and pain in the same way, but in this case, we should consider any individuals belonging to both those categories as moral agents.

Equating animals and humans in the context of moral agents would imply the recognition of direct duties toward both of them, while the Kantian distinction between direct and indirect duties would be unreasonable and unjustified.

Regan also states that the duty to abstain from causing suffering to a moral agent, as set out by Kant, would require taking into account only the capacity of suffering experienced by the subject, while it would be completely irrelevant whether or not its intellectual faculties are developed to a certain minimum level.

According to Regan, Kant's theory would lead us to conclude that human patients are ends in themselves, rather than simple means, or that they are things and, as such, instrumental with respect to moral agents.[56]

The conclusions reached by the contemporary Contractualist John Rawls are similar to those of Kant; discussing the categories of moral agents and moral patients, he concluded that it would not be mandatory for the first to take into account the consequences of their actions on the second.[57]

Since only moral agents are beneficiaries of direct duties, Rawls states that animals, belonging to the category of moral patients, cannot have rights and that, therefore, human beings, as moral agents, cannot have duties toward them.

Yet, despite the logical conclusion of his theories leading to an affirmation that there are no duties toward animals, the same Rawls argues that humans would nevertheless have obligations to nonhumans and that it is, in particular, *"definitely a bad thing to be cruel to animals and the destruction of a whole species can be a very serious damage."*[58]

Rawls called such duties *natural duties*, like those that he considers the source of mutual obligations arising from the social contract among moral agents.

In particular, according to Rawls, the ability to experience pleasure and suffering by animals would determine human duties not to cause suffering and to take into account the wellness of those animals.

Regan also detects criticalities of Rawls's view. In the first place, the human duty to not cause suffering to animals would appear to be a natural duty (the law of nature). In any case, Regan argues, Rawls also stated that natural duties may be associated exclusively to moral agents.

It would be contradictory to say that persons have duties toward animals and that, however, the latter do not belong to the category of moral agents nor to that of moral patients; therefore, Regan argues one of two things: animals should be considered moral agents or patients, or they cannot be considered beneficiaries of any duty.

Finally, Regan argues that the neocontractualist would leave unexplained and unproven one of the key topics of his moral theory; in fact, why should original contractors care about recognizing duties toward animals, being aware that they will never be in that category (of things), and being able to be exclusively in the state of moral agents, or in that of moral patients?

Moral Agents, Moral Patients, and the Cumulative Argument

After making a critical analysis of the most important philosophical current moral theories, and not agreeing with their conclusions, Regan outlines his philosophical theory, starting from defining what he means by the terms "*moral agent*" and "*moral patient*" as follows:

> Moral agents are individuals who have multiple and sophisticated capabilities, including in particular that of impartial moral principles to orientate the determination of what, all things considered, you have to do morally, as well as the ability, once accomplished this determination, to freely choose to act, or not, in accordance with morality, as they conceive it. Normal and adult humans are a typical example of individuals considered moral agents.[59]

As for the moral patients:

> Unlike moral agents, patients lack the moral prerequisites that would be necessary for them to control their own behavior and be accountable for their actions. The moral patients lack the ability to formulate moral principles, as well as taking inspiration by them when deciding what, among a number of possible multiple acts, would be right or proper to do. In a word, the moral patients cannot do what is right nor what is wrong. [...] The infants, young children, and members of the human species, at any age, presenting disabilities or mental deficiencies, are typical cases of human moral patients.[60]

Unlike moral agents, moral patients can present a variety of moral duties that would go from the mere possession of awareness or sentience, to the maturation of beliefs and memories of the past.

According to Regan, the argument traditionally used by detractors of the theory of animal rights, that, being unable to speak, they would have lower cognition and intellectual abilities than humans, is unfounded. He argues that the same attitude to the apprehension of language demonstrates the existence of a kind of pre-verbal awareness that makes it possible, and that, existing in humans, must also exist in nonhumans.

Regan attributes the animals' cognitive faculties to experiential data borrowed from science and evolutionism. Due to the common biological origin of human and nonhuman animals, it would seem a stretch to say that only humans have the capacity of self-understanding and comprehending the surrounding environment, and all the others do not.

The variety of skills in different species should be considered only quantitative but not qualitative— man might have more self-awareness than other animals, but this cannot be considered an exclusive prerogative.

Regan means to explain why nonhuman animals should be considered, in moral terms, similar to humans; to do so, he uses what he calls *Cumulative Argument*: a number of considerations which, once added to each other, should make his conclusions irrefutable:

1. *is in the common sense of people to attribute consciousness to certain animals;*
2. *in current language, the attribution of consciousness to animals is widespread;*
3. *there is no link between soul and conscience;*
4. *the observation of animal behavior confirms that they have conscience;*
5. *the Theory of Evolution provides a scientific representation of the reasons why nonhuman animals possess a conscience.* [61]

The first argument, based on social observation, emphasizes that people recognize, at least in some animals, the presence of a conscience, and this observation is inextricably linked to the second argument, which argues not only that it is a widespread mentality to consider some animals conscious, but also that when talking about animals, we usually make frequent reference to this prerogative.

The third argument, much more abstract and general, takes into account an issue often debated: do animals have a soul?

The question still occupies religions on different levels, as well as philosophies, and the answers are varied. Those who asked the question meant to determine whether or not animals can be considered holders of rights and, in particular, if it is possible to equate them to humans, who are traditionally considered the only owners of souls in the major religions.

Regan argues that the controversy surrounding animals' souls is meaningless because what really matters is consciousness, and consciousness has nothing to do with the soul; even if it were possible to demonstrate that nonhumans have no soul, it is still impossible to deny their conscience.

Of course, not everyone agrees about the consciousness of animals, and, indeed, Descartes founded a school of thought that denied animal consciousness on empirical basis, claiming that they were simply machines incapable of intellectual mechanisms. [62]

According to Regan it would be impossible to deny that animals are conscious, simply observing them—the behavior, the unique characteristics that each individual possesses, as well as their reactions, however different, to stresses, are so evident that it is impossible to doubt. Regan founds his fourth argument on this basis.

Beyond philosophical dissertations on the subject, in his fifth argument, Regan attests that after Darwin it is no longer possible to deny that animals are conscious, as this would have been scientifically proven, and if, in fact, our origin is the same as theirs, there is no reason to assume such a difference. [63]

Critique of Singer and Animal Rights

In *The Case for Animal Rights* (1983) Regan expresses his intention to reach the philosophical affirmation of the existence of real animal rights; before that, he builds an argumentative system based on the examination of Singer's work, which had been considered the most important philosophical doctrine in favor of animals.

The criticism of Singer's philosophy starts from the opinion that he would have concentrated on the wrong subject, considering benefits from actions rather than the subjects, and this, in Regan's view, would undermine the possibility of a complete protection of animals, leaving them perpetually exposed to potential abuse, as long as consequences remain advantageous to the agent.

In short, in Regan's view, Singer would always override the animals when doing so might represent a benefit for humans. [64]

In particular, Regan notes that, in disregarding the right to life of those subjects that cannot have expectations for the future, Singer contradicts himself—in that way, it would be impossible to cast blame for the killing of animals of which we ignore the mental abilities.

Also, the starting premise, that the self-conscious animals would be able to represent their future and have expectations, would be unproven, or at least questionable.

It seems that Regan correctly highlights the main intrinsic limits of Singer's thought: the assessment of interests, involving others, makes it impossible to apply a principle of real equality, as who acts will always have margins of arbitrariness.

Regan's thought represents a clean break with Singer, since the first denies the assumptions on which utilitarianism is based, that he considered to be insufficient and incapable of achieving a complete theory of animal rights.

In Regan's view, the principle of substitution represents the main limit of utilitarianism; to affirm that the creation of new individuals could compensate for the killing of some would allow actions conflicting with the instances of moral subjects.

Regan also challenges the principle of equality, another cornerstone of utilitarian thought. He argues that such philosophy does not imply it at all. Treating different subjects in a similar way does not necessarily mean one is treating them properly, or according to morals, but might mean that everyone received the same damage.[65]

Singer himself would deny the relevance of the principle of equality, stating that only the utility can be considered as the foundation of morality; that assertion, characteristic of utilitarianism, however, would deprive the importance of the principle of equality.

The conceptual distance between the principles of utility and equality would be underlined by Singer himself, when he admits that the utilitarian ideal would represent only a starting point, a sort of minimum essential[66] ; but this would be incompatible with utilitarianism, which, however, gives a fundamental importance to utility.

Moving from the general to the particular, Regan focuses on the issue of vegetarianism, stating that Singer's arguments are inconsistent, lacking philosophical relevant arguments, and also disregarding the basis of utilitarianism.

First Singer, stating that the sensory satisfaction from the consumption of meat represents a futile pleasure, should demonstrate something that Regan finds hard to recognize, as for anyone, utility, relevance, or pleasure are different and that, therefore, it is impossible to state in advance the futility of such interests.

Moreover, the criticism of the farms, based on the consideration that they do not bear significant utility, confuses the objectives with the consequences: the objective would be to provide contentment, while the consequence would be that all operators in the sector could survive thanks to that.

Taking into account the real consequences, rather than the objectives, it should be concluded that the interest in survival of meat producers represents a value very similar to that of animal life, if not superior to it, to the extent in which the human subjects are considered morally more important than their animal counterparts.[67]

Singer was also expected to demonstrate, on the basis of exact calculations, how the abolition of the farms could lead to a general improvement in well-being and that, therefore, the global situation following the adoption of a vegetarian diet is considerable utilitarian as the best or most consistent with morality: without such demonstrations vegetarianism in a utilitarian view is unfounded.

Nor would it be acceptable to base the defense of vegetarianism on the consideration that the increase in the number of vegetarians may lead to the closure of existing farms or preclude the opening of new ones; in fact, if it could be shown that the number of vegetarians is insufficient to determine similar effects, then utilitarianism cannot justify such a choice; that should actually be considered irrelevant.

Finally, Regan argues, even where the absolute number of vegetarians was sufficient to determine the changes, nothing would prevent an increase of carnivores or of meat consumption on the part of those existing, that would nullify any effort, making the change morally unjustifiable even in this case.

Regan states that the main limit of utilitarianism toward animals is the evaluation of happiness or well-being: due to its subjectiveness, it cannot be used as a valid parameter, except, possibly, in borderline cases. Outside of marginal hypothesis, in which the interests involved have measures macroscopically and objectively different, it would be difficult to argue whether a practice or an act could determine more well-being or frustration; on the contrary, it may be possible to justify a large number of behaviors with high damage potential, when an agent is unable to understand the damage suffered by others, or where he overestimated their well-being.

As a corollary of all his critical remarks of the utilitarian philosophy in general, and that of Singer in particular, Regan argues that the failure of such thinking is obvious, considering the condition of the animals and their treatment even after the dissemination of Singer's ideas; not only would there have been no revolution, but in many cases, the kinds of exploitation would have been increased.

In Regan's view, the failure of Singer's utilitarianism has deep roots in the lack of a genuine theory of animal rights. Without such recognition it would be impossible to establish and articulate their real safeguards against the abuses committed by human beings.

A prerequisite for the grant of rights to nonhuman animals would be the recognition of their value as individuals, which Regan describes as *inherent value*; this argument would be opposed to the typical utilitarianism, which recognizes importance to parties only in relation to their experiences, intended as memories of the past, expectations for the future, and awareness of events.

The inherent value would not be changed by the actions or thoughts of anyone, neither could be increased or decreased according to any benefit or utility; denying this, according to Regan, would mean to confuse the ends with the means.

One of the fears expressed along with the recognition of animal rights is that they could be considered equal to, or even placed before human beings. How should people act, in case of the need to choose between their own salvation and that of an animal?

In some criminal laws there is an exemption called "state of necessity": no one may be punished for an offense committed in such circumstances. The case par excellence is that of the survivor on a lifeboat, who survives by feeding off his companion.

How should the moral duty to refrain from killing animals as stated by Regan be applied in relation to the abovementioned case? Apparently, in the same way of the so-called "state of necessity," as Professor Regan, once asked, confirmed to me: *"Giving one's life in such circumstances would be supererogatory, not obligatory, so it's a matter of respect for the rights of nonhuman animals."* So, as you might not expect that a human sacrifice his own life for another human being, you might also not require that he save the life of a nonhuman animal at the cost of his own.

Subjects-of-a-life and the Principle of Respect

After clarifying that the inherent value is an absolute characteristic that can be wholly owned or not owned at all, but not partially, Regan questions the correct method to identify those who possess it; a possible criterion would be to attribute inherent value to anyone who lives, but Regan concludes that this would lead to results difficult to justify.

If any living thing were comparable, Regan argues, we should protect a blade of grass like cancer cells, like animals, and human beings; that statement does not seem reasonable, and therefore, Regan creates a real new category, which he identifies as *subjects-of-a-life*.[68]

Subjects-of-a-life, according to Regan, are all mammals one year old or more, in normal development.

The philosopher confesses to be perfectly aware of the difficulties occurring in an attempt to determine what the minimum threshold of self-determination is to consider an individual included in the category of new creation and, in this regard, he states that it is preferable to err on the excess rather than deficit, given that this criterion represents the dividing line for the validity of moral precepts.[69]

To prevent misunderstandings, Regan compares humans and nonhumans, to show that both have intellectual faculties, but also beliefs and desires, that would be the basis of real interests worthy of protection.

Regan adopts the concept of inherent value to identify the principle at the basis of the respect due to subjects-of-a-life and states that: *"All individuals who have inherent value have it equally, whether they are agents or moral patients."*[70]

Both moral agents and patients have inherent value, and the distinction, in Regan's view, must be made on the basis of belonging to the category of subjects-of-a-life:

> Individuals, namely, are subjects-of-a-life if they have beliefs and desires, perception, memory, sense of the future (even of their own future), an emotional life, as well as feelings of pleasure and pain, interests-preferences and interests-well-being, ability to initiate action in view of the gratification of their desires and the achievement of their objectives, psychophysical identity over time, and individual well-being in the sense that their life experience is positive or negative to them in terms logically independent from their being useful for others and their being of interest to anyone else. Those who meet the criteria of subject-of-a-life have a specific type of value—the inherent value—and they should not be considered or treated as mere receptacles[71]

It might be asked what space, in the theory of the subjects-of-a-life, environmental issues have, and if plants can somehow be considered right-holders. I asked Professor Regan that very question and he explained it this way: *"Individuals who are subjects-of-a-life have basic moral rights. Being a subject-of-a-life is a sufficient condition of such rights. I leave it an open question as to whether it is a necessary condition. That is, do living without a subject have rights? I leave this question open. My position basically is, 'Give me the argument for recognizing rights in non-sentient nature and let me think about it.' So far, no one has convinced me."* So Regan does not exclude absolutely the possibility of recognizing rights, even outside the animal kingdom, but he believes that there are no arguments to make it suitable so far.

The conceptual distinctions that Regan uses to recognize a different dignity to the environment and to animals could be intended as an expression of an empathic perception. The most similar to man, in short, would own more rights precisely because of that similarity. In fact, the answer that Regan provided me confirms that the recognition of rights to the subjects-of-a-life moves from those of humans: *"To recognize the rights of any nonhuman would be an extension of rights from the human. That being so, it seems reasonable to me that one accepts that this is what one is trying to do, which is why it is reasonable to begin with non-speciesist bases of human rights. Or I could put it this way: if human animals do not have rights, I can't see that there is some argument that could prove that nonhuman animals have rights."*

All subjects-of-a-life are recipients of moral rights, which, in his works, Regan argues to be distinguished from legal rights for being:

1. *innate;*
2. *universal;*
3. *equal.*[72]

According to the first prerogative, moral rights disregard any legislative action of creation; the legislature may only recognize them, but cannot create them.

Because of universalizability, moral rights belong to each individual of the same condition, while any form of discrimination has to be avoided.

According to Regan, moral rights are fundamental rights, not acquired; in that sense, there is a clear contrast with Bobbio, who considered it impossible to affirm the existence of fundamental or absolute rights outside those provided by the law.

Which is the basis of right, therefore, according to Regan? He, in answer to the question of what is the criterion informant at the base of morality, replied: "*Fundamentally, the right to be treated with respect. Derivatively, the rights to life, bodily integrity, and liberty.*"

Regan identifies the principle of respect with the *prima facie* duty not to harm any individual who is capable of experiencing well-being—this principle cannot be violated even in the case that it can bring benefits to others.

Regan argues that the principle of respect should be considered just the limit of the negative behavior toward moral patients; nothing below this would be allowed.

According to Regan, only the principle of respect would represent the innate belief that it is wrong to inflict pain, suffering, or death, both to moral agents or patients.

Enunciation of Direct Rights and Duties

In line with his critique of utilitarian morality, Regan formulates a philosophy of rights and duties based on inherent value, and, therefore, on absolute principles. The basis of these principles is the conception of animals as moral patients, as opposed to humans, who would rather be moral agents.

After establishing the minimum standard of respect, how should moral agents behave toward moral patients? To answer this question, Regan presents his theories of rights and duties.

The fundamental right is to be treated with respect, and it is owned both by moral agents and patients; this formulation clearly excludes the contractualist basis of right, since Regan also argues that patients do not possess the self-consciousness that represents the minimum requirement for the external-ization of a will, and, therefore, to adhere to the social contract.

In short, moral patients are neither morally good nor morally evil, neither innocent nor guilty, but nevertheless have intrinsic value, and therefore have the right to be treated with respect and to not be damaged. [73]

Next to the figure of rights, Regan also outlines that of duties, stating that they are also innate.

The fundamental duty, according to Regan, is that of justice; unless there are differences in moral terms, it is necessary to recognize to each what is due to him in the same way and without arbitrary distinctions. [74]

Overcoming what he considers to be a fundamental limitation of Singer's philosophy, Regan specifies that all persons who have inherent value have the right to claim a treatment inspired by the criterion of respect, and when this claim is frustrated, they would be entitled to complain.

If it is true that nobody should normally cause damage to any person who possesses inherent value, it is also true that this is not always possible in reality, and that, therefore, one can occasionally be forced to determine what subject is preferable to damage, being unable to avoid causing damage alto-gether.

According to Regan, from the principle of respect arises the principle of *minimization of violations*—between two groups of individuals whose dam-age is similar, one should choose to damage the numerically smaller.

On the other hand, the damage would not always be comparable and, therefore, a situation where a group is most damaged of another as a result of a specific behavior may occur. In this case, Regan argues, the numerical principle inspired by the minimization of violations should be overruled by the principle of the most disadvantaged. [75] This means that it is preferable to damage a larger group, whenever its damages are lower than those that would result to another group.

Regan argues that his theory of justice, unlike utilitarianism, overcomes discrimination.

Regan shows a few examples of the above, comparing both groups of humans who are different from each other, and human to nonhuman animals; in the first case, utilitarianism justifies (or would justify) racial discrimina-tion, as, for example, a group of whites could legitimately cause harm to a group of blacks, since the connected advantage derived would be quantita-tively greater than the harm caused.

Just as with racism among humans, even speciesism toward animals would find legitimacy in the utilitarian perspective for the same reasons; by contrast, Regan argues that between an animal and a human being with disabilities there is no morally relevant difference and that, therefore, all that can be justified in one case must also be justified in the other. [76]

Animal Rights and Vegetarianism/Veganism

As a corollary of his theories, Regan states what behaviors humans should adopt with nonhumans, considering vegetarianism fundamental. He does not consider that a possibility, but a duty, as an expression of the principle of respect and duty of justice.

In Regan's words, there is a firm condemnation of all forms of eating animals, so much so that he says: "*From the moral point of view, the practice of raising animals for food purposes must cease.*"[77]

Regan sees no difference between intensive and extensive farming, since, unlike the utilitarian perspective, he believes that the amount of suffering caused is not important, but simply the violation of rights connected with any form of animal exploitation for food, without distinction.

Particularly, Regan addresses an appeal to the people who can make a difference, not only by being vegetarian, but in "*helping to educate those who are currently supporting the animal industry, so that they realize the implications of their support, and helping to credit the view that this industry, as we know it, violates the animal rights and, if necessary, to work because the force of law compel the industry to make the necessary changes [...]. Settling for personally refraining from meat would mean becoming part of the problem rather than part of the solution.*"[78]

Regan is aware that the average mentality criticizes vegetarianism, and he considers it necessary to systematically argue, to prove the groundlessness, and, therefore, to affirm the moral necessity that humans stop eating animals.

Usually people criticize vegetarianism/veganism on the basis of the so-called *law of nature*, according to which every animal could overwhelm the weaker. Is that view correct? Regan told us that: "*We do not accept such an ethic when it comes to how humans should treat one another. Why should we accept this kind of ethic when we ask how nonhumans should be treated? My answer is: we should not.*"

In addition to the references to the *law of nature*, the general principle that inspires the defense of the omnivorous diet is "freedom." Those who argue believe in a person's right to choose his food and, at the same time, a right to non-interference by others.

The affirmation of the principle of freedom in the practice of breeding animals or in their consumption would be possible, Regan argues, only in the case that it were possible to see in all the prerogatives of the principle of liberty, opportunity, which he denies, contemplating each argument in an analytical way.[79]

The most used arguments against vegetarianism/veganism are of two types: on one hand, in favor of sensory satisfaction, and, on the other hand, those of economic nature.

The omnivores' justifications:

1. giving up meat would deprive them of a satisfaction;
2. the personal habits and cultural push to consume meat and give it up would lead to problems and hard changes;
3. abstaining from meat consumption would be detrimental to health.

Regan easily refutes the first argument, pointing out that giving up a sensory pleasure cannot be compared to the deprivation of life inflicted on animals. In addition, he says, it would not even be fair to say that foregoing the consumption of meat causes the deprivation of pleasure derived from food, since this can clearly also be obtained from a plant-based food.

The second argument represents a problem of lower rank than the damage that animals undergo, as even in this case it would not be possible to equate morally, or even simply compare, the pain resulting from the consumption of meat with the hypothetical suffering from the change.

The objection about the risks to health is, in the opinion of Regan, scientifically unfounded. There would be no need to partake of flesh to live a healthy lifestyle, as the same substances are contained in plant foods.

The second set of arguments against vegetarianism regards the prospect of farmers and, in general, the economic operators involved with the production process[80] :

1. the production of meat sustains a certain part of the human population;
2. the entire economic system of each country is benefited by the meat industry;
3. producers and breeders exercise animals' legal rights;
4. certain animals would not be included among those protected under the theory of rights;
5. farm animals are created by the will of farmers and, therefore, their lives are entrusted to them;
6. the principle of the most disadvantaged would give farmers the right to exploit animals because they would be the more disadvantaged otherwise.

Regan contends that the first argument would be denied because each entrepreneur assumes the risk of free enterprise and cannot in any way claim the right to be supported in this by other parties, nor recognize the duty of consumers to support; moreover, the principle of respect requires boycotting businesses that involve the systematic violation, what would be, in fact, the breeding of animals for food.

As for the employees of this industry, those who have not chosen either the activity or the business risk, Regan argues that it is impossible to say that people have any sorts of duty, since just states, or, in any case, public entities, would be responsible.

The second argument would be rejected like the first, based on the fact that no one can claim a right to harm others and that, therefore, any person participating in an economic system based on the infliction of suffering and death, has no right to claim a sort of protection from other people.

Regan says that to give practical application to the theory of rights and, therefore, to the principle of respect, is a duty that cannot be ignored, even if fulfilling it requires revolutionization of the economic system.[81]

The right to property related to the fourth argument would be, according to Regan, not unlike that which affirmed the legality of slavery in relation to other human beings and that, with the evolution of thought, has been repealed; in the same way, the theory of animal rights' goal is precisely to extend their status as subjects of rights.

The fact that farm animals exist only because they are created by the will of the breeders would also lead to a significant reduction in their number—according to Regan, a highly desirable circumstance—and that, even among humans, means better life conditions.[82]

Exposing his position compared to the fourth argument, Regan interprets his own theory: first, he points out that it is not easy to distinguish who belongs to the category of subjects-of-a-life and, therefore, in the absence of certainties, it is necessary to adopt the criterion of maximum security and caution, ensuring also to animals, like roosters and hens, the respect due to the subjects-of-a-life.

Notwithstanding that, strictly defined, only mammals over one year of age would be considered as subjects-of-a-life; the exclusion does not only concern the different species, such as chickens and hens, but also in the case of puppies and other mammals. In this case, Regan admits that there would be no way to include them in the group of subjects-of-a-life, but he also notes that this condition would be transient and, therefore, there would be a legitimate expectation to be protected.[83]

The fifth argument derives from a patriarchal culture that attributed to the father the right of life and death over his children and that is no longer considered valid by our culture; as we should apply the same considerations related to men to animals, the most logical conclusion would be to reject that argument, uniformly for human and nonhuman animals.

The sixth argument is not, according to Regan, less unfounded than the previous. The reference to the principle of the most disadvantaged, in fact, might make sense only in the case that all individuals involved are treated with respect.[84]

Since no type of farming for food can be considered compatible with respect for the animals, Regan concludes that, in any case, the principle of the most disadvantaged cannot provide any valid justifications to farmers.

Also, considering animals as replaceable resources would be unacceptable. In this way, they would be vulnerable to any arbitrariness by their owners, totally disregarding the principle of respect and denying the inherent value of animals.

1.4 GARY FRANCIONE AND THE ABOLITIONIST APPROACH

Background and Critical to Singer and Regan

Professor Gary L. Francione, the first American University Professor of animal rights, distinguishes himself from the most illustrious philosophers of animal rights, being also a lawyer, who has practiced law and clerked.[85]

Francione's formation in the law particularly characterizes his thoughts and work toward the legal issues of animal rights; in this sense, it can be said that he is marked to pragmatism, as demonstrated by his personal attention to the protection of animals.

Francione, through his own page on the social network Facebook[86], informs about theoretical aspects and daily shares information about adoptions of stray animals in New York, that, after being collected on the street, are subject to death by inhalation of carbon monoxide in special gas chambers.

Francione himself defines his theory "the abolitionist approach," and this definition is also the name of the website that he has dedicated to information and discussion.[87]

Francione's abolitionism is perfectly expressed by Gary Steiner in Francione's *Animals as Persons* (foreword): *Essays on the Abolition of Animal Exploitation*:

> Abolitionists [...] see any such uses of animals as a fundamental violation of their right not to be property, and they argue that all uses of animals to satisfy human desires must cease altogether. Francione argues that we have no moral justification for continuing to bring domestic animals into existence for human use. One focal point of his work has been his effort to demonstrate that there are now more animal welfare regulations in place than ever before, and yet there is more exploitation inflicted on more animals today than ever before[88]

Francione's view about animal rights is well represented in his 1995 book *Animals, Property, and The Law*. This is probably the best summary of the two souls coexisting in Francione: on the one hand, the philosophical formation, which leads to the discussion of theoretical arguments, and, on the other hand, the jurist who examines concrete cases and expresses criticisms and proposals about positive law.

In all his works, and on all media channels, Francione emphasizes the centrality of veganism. Where his predecessors had spoken, in more general terms, of vegetarianism, Francione uses the term "veganism" instead.

Francione took the distances from both Singer and Regan, for different reasons, although based on the same consideration; neither would be able to establish a philosophy of animal rights free of inconsistencies, and the result would be precisely the lack of concrete solutions in the treatment of animals.

The criticism against Singer is a critique of utilitarianism, considered unable to create theoretical tools necessary for the proper affirmation of animal rights.

About Singer, Francione argues:

> My analysis differs from that of Peter Singer who, in Animal Liberation, maintains that our use of nonhumans may be morally acceptable if we ensure that animals have reasonably pleasant lives and relatively painless deaths. I maintain that we have no moral justification for treating animals as replaceable resources—as our property—however 'humanely' we may treat them or kill them[89]

Francione believes that the idea that Singer is an animal rights advocate is the result of a misunderstanding, as he has never made any statement on the subject of animal rights; like all philosophers belonging to utilitarianism, Singer gives relevance only to the consequences of actions, and, therefore, he disagrees with the concept of moral rights.

After making a preliminary clarification, Francione reviews Singer's arguments, starting with the belief that animals have no sense of time, nor expectations for the future, and, therefore, that they cannot be damaged by death; for this reason, Singer focuses on their treatment, whereas it is essential that they do not suffer, while he views their death as secondary, or even irrelevant.

According to Singer, only humans have a self-consciousness that justifies their interest to live, but Francione argues that such an assumption is unproven, and, therefore inadmissible. The differences between human and nonhuman self-consciousness, he states, can certainly exist, as indeed they are present even among healthy adult men and who, by age or due to trauma or disease, may have lost memory or part of their mental faculties.

Is it possible to distinguish sentient beings on the basis of self-consciousness? According to Francione, who opposes Singer on the question, the answer is negative. The fact of being sentient would be a mere instrument that nature has given to animals to protect their lives, and, therefore, we should conclude that all those who have the instrument must also share the end, namely the prolongation of life.

The question of animals' treatment, in Singer's view, however, would be problematic for other reasons. First, determining what can be classified as abuse involves a complicated comparison of suffering. Francione argues that this would not be easy, even if all the subjects involved were humans, while assuming something that cannot be directly experienced is unreasonable and unprovable.

Francione's analysis highlights a significant limitation of Singer's philosophy: basing a system of values on suffering requires one to assume a method of evaluation and comparison of well-being and suffering, before we can determine which is the most moral action.

In Singer's thought, the principle of equal consideration of interests is fundamental, while Francione believes that this is not applied in respect to animals; on the other hand, he says that it would have been necessary to challenge the legal status of animals as property, to ensure the actual equal consideration of their interests as opposite to human interests.

Even in this case, Francione's critical consideration seems correct—the equal consideration of interests would require that animals are free to realize their expectations and their own nature, outside of the constraints and impositions of humans. Stating that nonhumans' interests count like those of humans, but restricting them in the number and in the extent of such would be illogical and would ultimately claim the opposite principle, namely, that human interests (ownership, entertainment, etc.) prevail over those of nonhumans.

Francione's position, far away from utilitarianism, is certainly more similar to deontologism and to Regan's view; the main point of contact between Regan and Francione is the adherence to the principle of animal rights, while both are opposed to Singer's view.

While there are some similarities between Regan and Francione, it would be wrong to consider that the latter fully shares the first's ideas—far from that, Francione underlined several of Regan's contradictions.

> Francione clarifies his similarities and differences with Regan, stating that: In The Case for Animal Rights, Tom Regan also argues against animal welfare and regulation and in favor of animal rights and abolition. But my view and Regan's differ. Regan links the concept of being a subject-of-a-life, a notion focusing on cognitive characteristics beyond mere sentience and requiring a sort of preference autonomy, or the ability to satisfy preferences and not merely to have interests. Although Regan says that being a subject-of-a-life is a sufficient and not necessary condition for being morally significant. His theory is based in important respects on cognitive characteristics beyond sentience[90]

The main criticism concerns the conceptual category of the subjects-of-a-life, that, according to Francione, is elaborate, superfluous, and irrelevant to the formulation of a system of animal rights, as well as inconsistent for many reasons.

Francione wonders how it is possible to exclude from the subjects-of-a-life animals such as fish or birds, which science has proven to be sentient, as well as that they possess those skills that Regan attributed exclusively to mammals. The conclusion is that the distinction is arbitrary, and, therefore, inadmissible in a coherent philosophical theory.

Francione's arguments seem valid and conclusive; although Regan has stated that the exclusion from the list of subjects-of-a-life does not imply the absence of moral duties, it is still evident—and Regan admits as much—that the distinction is completely arbitrary.

In addition to the vice of arbitrariness there would be one, even worse, of inconsistency. The equality of all subjects-of-a-life should determine the equalization in all respects and in all circumstances, while Regan does not bring his own theory to the logical conclusion, given that when he compared humans and animals in an emergency situation, the first always prevail.

The controversial example of the lifeboat clarifies Regan's view. In the case in which four humans and a dog are on a lifeboat and you have to choose which of them to throw out of the boat for the salvation of the others, according to Regan, it would be correct to save the humans.

The choice of saving humans is based on the conviction that a dog's death represents a lesser evil, compared to that of a man, so much that even millions of dogs would be expendable to save a single human being.[91] Francione argues that this conclusion is not consistent with the premises, as it betrays a speciesist perspective, rather than a real equal consideration of all the subjects-of-a-life.

Indeed, Francione states even Singer found the criticality of Regan's conclusions, considering that the example of the lifeboat demonstrates how the position of the latter is theoretically able to justify any exploitation of animals by humans, recognizing an incontestable superiority toward humans in the comparison of interests.[92]

Even in this case, Francione's conclusion seems correct: the conceptual equivalence of all subjects-of-a-life is in fact nullified by Regan's conclusions, since, after that, he put the dog on the same rank of humans, yet then he moves it further down again, considering the dog expendable to save the man.

Finally, the most important question that, according to Francione, Regan misses, is the legal status of animals and, in this regard, the first states that the second would not have accomplished his thoughts on animal rights, failing to take a stand for the abolition of the status of things.

Critical to the Legal Status of Animals and to Welfarism

One of the main criticisms that Francione has advanced with regard to both Singer and Regan is the fact that neither has ever openly condemned the status of nonhumans as things.

According to Francione, in Western societies, the exploitation of nonhumans is allowed at any level because they are considered as property from all legal systems, and, therefore, they are no different from any other object.

The demonstration of the connection between animals and economy passes through the etymological analysis of the Latin term "pecunia," which indicates money and derives from "pecus," meaning "cattle." The root has been maintained unchanged in meaning, even in the English-speaking world, which also uses the world "capital" that comes from "cattle."[93]

Francione clarifies the importance of the animal status:

> The property status of animals [...] acts as a blinder that effectively blocks even our perception of their interests as similar to ours because any limitation on property owners is understood to represent significant human "suffering." And even in those instances in which human and animal interests are recognized as similar, animals will lose in any balancing of interests because the property status of animals is always a good reason not to accord similar treatment unless to do so would benefit property owners[94]

Francione, who inspired all his works to the principle of abolition of animals' legal status of property, took into account the criticisms that have been made by other thinkers, such as Professor Sunstein. Sunstein claims that the status of property should not be necessarily eliminated, and also that it would better protect nonhumans.

Sunstein's thesis is that the owners of domestic animals do not treat them as objects, but as living beings; moreover, the protection would be provided by the law, that provides owners' obligations, duties, and responsibility.[95]

Francione opposes three arguments to Sunstein's considerations:

1. Sunstein would refer exclusively to domestic animals, and, therefore, his thought may be applied only with respect to a limited series of all possible relationships between humans and nonhumans;
2. in each case, with reference to the limited number of reports included in Sunstein's analysis, the fact that owners decide to treat animals well is completely based on their will and when this does not occur, the law protects owners' rights;
3. the third and final, but substantial, problem is that the same ratio of domestication, introduced and maintained by humans, according to Francione, is to be morally condemned. As long as men choose to bring animals into existence at their will, it will be inevitable to make choices that require them to evaluate and contrast the interests of different species.

From the considerations about animals' legal status, Francione derives his theory of *moral schizophrenia*, stating that it regards both relations, between humans and nonhumans.

If, on the one hand, humans often declare themselves interested in the animals' welfare or claim to love animals, on the other side, they perform all kinds of abuse. The reference is to practice, which is increasingly of selective interest for some nonhuman species or certain interspecies relationships, while, at the same time, participating in practices that, directly or indirectly, cause death and suffering to other species or individuals.

A typical example of moral schizophrenia toward animals is to consider a dog as a family member and a pig as food, as well as to protect the so-called pet from abuse, yet still allowing that many species be used for very painful experiments.

The effect of moral schizophrenia would be the inability to ascribe to similar situations similar importance, and, therefore, the inability to recognize and truly protect animal rights.

Moral schizophrenia is reflected by a legislation based on welfarism, as opposed to the doctrine of rights.

About welfarism, Francione says: "*The animal welfare position, which holds that we may use nonhumans for human purposes, is the prevailing contemporary framework that governs our relationship with nonhumans. This position maintains that although we may use nonhumans, we have a moral and legal obligation to treat them 'humanely' and not to inflict 'unnecessary' suffering on them.*"[96]

The welfarist position is, at least in the context of the protection of animals, antithetical to abolitionism. According to Francione, it would not be conceivable to guarantee any improvement in the condition of nonhumans through laws inspired by this principle, and to prove it, he adopts an empirical approach based on examination of the laws adopted in recent decades and their effects.

The animal laws in the United States and United Kingdom, Francione argues, are based on welfarism, as they condemn the murder and ill-treatment, but only when considered "not necessary."

Unlike when such treatment is directed toward humans, the legislature does not establish an absolute animal right not to suffer ill-treatment nor to be killed, but only a right conditioned to the lack of an emergency, since in that case "needs" are intended just for humans.

Even in the case of crimes against other human beings, the state of necessity may be relieved of responsibility; then it would not be a new concept. What distinguishes the state of necessity relevant to humans from that relevant to nonhumans, according to Francione, is that, when applied to animals, it would not occur at all a real need, as the economic benefit always justifies any exploitation, including death.

The fact that animals are property and the moral schizophrenia that follows determines, as a result, derogations to the prohibition of the ill-treatment and killing to such an extent as to make them completely irrelevant and only applicable in numerically marginal cases.

The paradox of welfarism is that he who beats a dog on the street is punishable, while it is perfectly legal to kill an animal in a slaughterhouse, despite the fact that eating meat is not necessary to survive, according to Francione.

In short, comparing humans and nonhumans, the first have a prejudice that makes it impossible to apply the principle of equal consideration of interests; if it were not so, it would be impossible to explain why an interest as the right to life or to not being abused can be considered less important than the pleasure obtained from tasty food or watching a funny show, etc.

Francione concludes that is precisely the property status of animals to prevent the affirmation of the principle, theoretically recognized as valid by many, of equal consideration of interests; moving the animals from the category of things to that of moral subjects would finally emancipate them from the welfarist/speciesist perspective.

The rejection of welfarism for philosophical reasons induces Francione to challenge not only actual laws, but also the activity of many animal welfare organizations, which, by endorsing the thesis of the "humane exploitation," represent a threat to animal rights.

To substantiate its opposition to welfarism, Francione analyzes it based on the following statements:

1. *the animals are the property of humans. The difference between wild and domestic animals is that while the former are property of the community, the latter belong to specific individuals;*
2. *it is legitimate to use animals for human purposes;*
3. *any social practice is appropriate to establish the exploitation of animals;*
4. *the cruelty is rejected, only if it prevents animal exploitation.*

Francione argues that promoting welfarism diverts from the solution of animals' problems for several reasons: first, until the idea of animals as property is abandoned, it will be impossible to consider them as right-holders.

Moreover, spreading the belief that improving the exploited animal's conditions is a good thing would distract from their real needs, and, therefore, from achieving a concrete protection, possible only with the recognition of real rights.

In Francione's view, the welfarist legislation causes many despicable results:

1. *derogations from the system of protection include the most common animal exploitations and, therefore, protective laws are only marginally applicable;*
2. *the interpretation extended the derogations, to include a large number of additional circumstances not initially planned and, thus, admitting any practice;*
3. *most of the penalties assumes the agent's malice, but it is often not possible to provide such evidence;*
4. *there is a presumption that pet owners do not cause them more suffering than is necessary considerable, as this would be in their own interest;*
5. *the enforcement of laws to protect animals and, more importantly, the imposition of sanctions, are uneasy.*

In particular, about v), Francione points out that there is not a real social stigma against those who commit crimes against animals, because people would be reluctant to consider one who simply disposes of his property as a criminal. [97]

A further critical against welfarist legislation is that animals cannot take legal action and, therefore, it is possible to intervene and, if necessary, punish those responsible for ill-treatment only in the event that persons or groups promote the action.

The Abolitionism and the Equal Consideration of Interests

Excluding the theory of welfarism, Francione investigates the theory of rights and nature and basis of right, stating that every sentient being should have the right to not suffer because of someone else's will.

The affirmation of the fundamental right not to suffer does not end the discussion about animal rights, as it is only the beginning; the problem usually faced by the philosophers are the situations of conflict and their resolution. How should we behave in the face of a compelling threat to the life of a human being and that of an animal? Should we save the child or the dog? Who matters more?

According to Francione, sustaining animal rights does not mean that we assign them more value than humans, but rather, that we ensure that their interests are equalized—arguing that both are moral subjects, yet in case of conflict, the fact that humans prevail, represents an irreconcilable contradiction.

Francione often uses a parallelism between the modern condition of animals and human slaves, which was denied those rights possessed by their masters; such theories would then be the basis of racial discrimination, which prevent us from considering all subjects on the same level, giving them relevance on the basis of a prejudice.

Francione admits that he does not consider human rights as actually absolute, and that, indeed, it is often difficult to understand the purpose of rights protected by law; he concludes that in any case the rights based on respect can be compressed or limited only on consequentialist/utilitarian basis. [98]

The corollary of the above is that:

> In the lifeboat or burning-house situation, decide to favor the human over the nonhuman not because death is a lesser harm to the nonhuman, but because we do not know what death means to the nonhuman and we have a better idea what it means to the human. We might, therefore, rely on this—a matter of epistemological limitation on our part and not any empirical claim that death is a lesser harm to humans—as the tie-breaker that is on fire, we should decide to promote the human instead of the nonhuman because death is far less damage to the nonhuman, but since we do not know what death means for the nonhuman, and we have a better idea of what it means for the human. [...] In no case, however, would I think it appropriate to invoke any notion that humans are 'higher' animals [99]

In accordance with the principle of equal consideration of interests, Francione argues that the only possible conclusion is the abolitionism, which he contrasts with welfarism, stating that any form of animal exploitation must be considered morally illegitimate, and therefore be rejected.

The abolitionist approach, preventing any exploitation and use of animals, would preclude all practices of interaction among species based on the principle of the availability of nonhumans by humans—this does not imply only eating, experimentation, performances and shows, but also the domestication. [100]

The keeping of animals in our houses represent forms of use that are not compatible with the rights recognized to moral subjects and that, therefore, should cease.

Even the paradigmatic example of the burning-house and the choice between saving the child and the dog, from the abolitionist point of view, is examined from a different perspective: the dog, in fact, has not entered voluntarily into the house, and, therefore, those who put him there have the duty to save him, or avoid creating the conditions for the conflict in the first place.

The abovementioned example is, of course, an extreme case and is very unlikely to occur in everyday life. For this reason, Francione claims that it would be absurd to base a moral theory on such extreme circumstances; in such a case, the choice between human and nonhuman would be emotional, but it would be the same between individuals of the same species.

Francione argues that each individual, in a desperate situation in which they are forced to face an extreme choice and can save only one, will act on the basis of emotions and feelings that are subjective and arbitrary: one might decide to save the dog, because of loyalty, while the child is not his own, or one may choose to save his baby son at the expense of others.

Francione considers the example of the choice between humans and nonhumans a false problem that demonstrates one of the fears that society seems to have with respect to the recognition of animal rights; some fear that it would end up putting the interests of nonhumans before those of humans, or to recognize them the same rights.

Francione considers improbable that animal and human rights would become identical. It is impossible, for example, to extend the right to vote to animals, as it is for any other right that presupposes human skills, not owned by animals.

The only animal right definitely recognizable is not to be treated as objects, and to justify that, Francione examines the conflicting arguments, assuming that this right is due, unless proved otherwise.

The first criticism about animal rights is the Cartesian-based assumption, according to which they would not be conscious or sentient, but this would be easily refuted by empirical observation.

The second objection is religious and affirms that God would give man the right to exploit animals for their own interest. It is a widespread perception in the West and largely based on the interpretation of sacred Christian and Jewish texts.

The contractualist thought of Locke, which has greatly inspired the Western legal systems (especially Anglo-Saxon), is based precisely on the anthropocentric conception of Christianity, which legitimizes humans' right to use and exploit all creation.

Francione denies the moral acceptability of the anthropocentric perspective of religious derivation, stating that there are at least three good reasons to reject it:

1. accepting this theory would imply the need to accept all the other biblical statements about the origin of the world;
2. the interpretation that entitle humans to dispose of animals would be only one of those possible, since the assignment of the latter to the former does not necessarily imply the occurrence of any absolute right;
3. you might not admit the legality of animal exploitation without feeling equally applicable to all biblical precepts that lead to discriminatory behavior, for example against women and children, but also the legitimacy of slavery.

According to Francione, Darwinism has completely debunked this interpretation, making it impossible to support it nowadays. The naturalist, in fact, clearly explained that the cognitive differences between species are merely of degree and not of kind, and that, therefore, the hypothesis that humanity has a nature distinct from the rest of the animal kingdom has no scientific basis.

None of the distinguishing characteristics of human beings, Francione argues, is exclusive. First, any of their skill can be found in many other species, and, on the other hand, there are humans who do not possess them at all, such as babies, injured, etc.

The fourth argument against animal rights refer to some of Regan's thoughts, or at least to the interpretation that some (including Francione) have given: it would not be possible to deny that animals have inherent value, but that value would be lower than that of humans.

Francione argues that assigning a relative inherent value is erroneous and contradictory, since those who are considered to have less value could be automatically considered objects, in balancing with individuals considered to have more value.

The relativization of the inherent value would represent only a discrimination based on prejudice rather than an impartial reflection based on logic— in this way, as in the case of the argument of religious derivation, the result would be to legitimize and substantiate any discrimination (sexual, racial, etc.).

Critical to Eco-feminism

Alongside the more established traditional philosophical theories, Francione also considers other contemporary currents of thought about animals; one of these is the eco-feminism, a movement that refuses the principles of the patriarchal society, and, consequently, of all its implications.

According to eco-feminists, the theory of animal rights is misconceived in the first place because it would perpetuate the institution of the right, which is considered a patriarchal institute to be abolished.

Against the right theory, the eco-feminist movement opposes the *ethic of care*, namely a system that rejects any absolute and requires each case to be treated as a standalone, choosing from time to time the correct conduct to ensure respect for the other.

The rule of conduct could never be detached from individuals, and, therefore, could not be related to either a species or to a group as a whole; this should exclude discrimination and also makes unnecessary the use of general codified rights, which do not take into consideration the specificity.

Francione faces the eco-feminists criticism against the theory of animal rights, making an example: *"The ethic of care is relevant to deciding whether we should eat this particular animal or use this particular animal in an experiment only if the institutional exploitation of animals in science and agriculture is accepted as a general matter.*"[101]

Francione proposes again the parallelism between animal rights and human rights, with the example of slavery: *"We could not have had human slavery without first deciding that it was morally permissible to treat slaves as 'things,' as human property, rather than as persons who have at least some interests that are protected from being traded away for consequential reasons alone (in this case, benefit for the slave owners)."*[102]

Considering human slaves, Francione argues, it would have been unthinkable to criticize the institutionalized right to freedom, as it would not have been possible to achieve the same result using the ethic of care, based on individual relations. As human slavery, even the use of animals for food, experiments, and other types of exploitation, is the result of a social, as well as legal, construction that cannot be surpassed only considering isolated behaviors referred to specific individuals, but that requires a transformation of the same grade, and, namely, legal and social.

Finally, Francione argues that eco-feminists theories do not go beyond, as promised, the formulation of the theory of animal rights, but they simply challenge it without offering real alternatives, except intuitions isolated and without a systematic frame.

Francione's conclusion is that the ethic of care, even if it cannot be considered a complete theory, may nevertheless be usefulness, within the conceptual framework defined by the theory of animal rights, limited to the definition of a more defined minimum standard.

Apology of Veganism

"Veganism represents a rejection of the commodity status of nonhumans and a recognition of their inherent value."[103] With this lapidary statement, Francione clarifies the fundamental importance of veganism within the philosophy of animal rights, and, in particular, in his thought.

The importance of veganism goes beyond food issues, since, in Francione's view, it has an exceptional moral and political value, representing the starting point to change the relationships between humans and nonhumans, on the basis of respect.

The choice goes beyond the mere question of food because, as Francione explained, it implies a lifestyle that rejects not only eating animals, but also the use of clothing and accessories that require the exploitation of nonhumans.

Francione does not speak, generically, about "vegetarianism." He speaks exclusively in favor of veganism, stating that *"There is probably more suffering in a glass of milk or an ice-cream cone than there is in a steak."*[104]

Francione explains his opposition to vegetarianism, arguing that the animals exploited in the milk industry, while living longer than those intended for meat production, face living conditions far worse, and are not spared from the killing in slaughterhouses, which is the end of their production cycle.

Francione states that there are not interests even remotely comparable with the suffering and death inflicted, since the pleasure arising from the flavor of the food has a lower rank, and, unlike those not forced to suffer and prolong their existence, cannot be considered an absolute right.

From the above, Francione derives a total disapproval against those who call themselves "animal advocates," while continuing to eat animals; hence he builds another analogy between human slavery and the exploitation of nonhumans. *"That is no different from someone who claims to be in favor of the abolition of slavery but continues to own slaves."*[105]

Any movement that aspires to reduce the suffering of animals but does not firmly condemn their use for food, given the damage that such practice causes against billions of animals every year, is to be considered contradictory and unfounded.

Equally unfounded is the position of those who, like Singer, promote (or whatever consider right to promote) the consumption of meat in a responsible manner, for example, by reducing the consumption, and, anyway, through the choice of food products from non-intensive farming, which ensure the animals a life "happy" and free from abuses.

Francione's critique against people and associations that promote or allow the use of animals, as long as they are not abused, is also based on practical considerations: he assumes that the public is less offended by such campaigns rather than other, more radical, ones intended to affirm veganism.

Francione argues that the maximum limit of the use of concepts such as "conscious consumption" and "happy animals" is their incapacity to change the foundations of collective thought. Far from causing conversions, on the contrary, that would reassure consumers or aspiring vegetarians/vegans, making it impossible to understand the real implications of their choices.

Francione justifies his criticism against some animal welfare organizations' initiatives, claiming that if these organizations had promoted veganism the last thirty years instead of multiple campaigns aimed at reducing the suffering associated with the exploitation of various types, today the number of vegans in the world would be far higher; Francione also believes that the effectiveness of this single change in lifestyle is enough to produce a reduction of animal suffering far greater than the sum of all the other initiatives so far conducted.

Returning to the legal issue, which is closely linked to his work, Francione also considers the vegan choice essential to allow the formation of an economic and political substrate able to work toward the achievement of the legal changes necessary to the recognition of animal rights.

Upstream of any change in the legal system, there would be economic and political interests that, at present, are closely associated with the industry of the exploitation of animals and that, in order to be overwhelmed, should be offset by an equal interest. For this reason, the philosopher calls for a transformation in the way of thinking, which allows, in the longterm, the implementation of decisive changes, not limited to marginal aspects of the humans-nonhumans relationship.

Abolitionism's Perspectives

Francione, questioning prospects of abolitionism, investigates whether it is necessary to await the full realization before transposing animal rights into any legal form, or whether it is possible to achieve this result in advance; the conclusion is that it

> might be possible to build a pluralist system that considers animals as property but recognizing pseudo rights at some level. Therefore, though it does not make sense to talk about animal rights in our contemporary legal system if what you mean by rights is what Regan argues as rights, we may, however, be able to reach some kind of animal protection through some near-rights, a protection based on the recognition of the interests of animals that cannot be sacrificed solely on the basis of consequentialist considerations [106]

The instrument to achieve this sort of hybrid model between abolitionism, and, instead, the permanence of the current system of indiscriminate exploitation, according to Francione, lies in the use of specific tools such as legal institutes, not intended to "regulate," but to abolish, at least selectively.

According to Francione, any regulation can legitimize the exploitation, while selectively abolishing some methods of exploitation would allow the public to understand that forms of use that, properly regulated, are admissible cannot exist.

An example of selective or partial abolition would be the limitation of certain practices, such as specific experiments, designed to allow definite decrease in the number and variety of cruelty to animals, without legitimating any practices.

In support of the intermediate position, Francione states that any claim of a right is upheld when corresponding rules are set to refrain from all conducts prejudicial to the right; for such reason, the abolition of certain forms of ill-treatment is conceptually much more relevant and consistent than the mere disapproval of the forms of exploitation "inhumane," which would automatically legitimize all the others, considered "humane."

Moreover, provided that certain practices, such as experiments of a certain type, are unacceptable for any sentient being would represent a not insignificant achievement toward the affirmation of animal rights.

Insights

Professor Francione kindly answered some questions in the making of this work.

The first question concerns the argument, often adopted by non-vegetarians to challenge the theoretical basis of food choice that rejects the use of animals, based on the so-called law of nature, according to which it would be permissible to use other sentient beings for self purposes.

Is it therefore possible to consider justified the criticism based on the natural law? Professor Francione's response: "*No, of course not. First of all, there is a great deal of cooperation in nature. This nonsense about the 'strongest' prevailing is more relevant to the Social Darwinism that developed (and still exists) and has nothing to do with 'facts.'*"

Another issue that has been the focus of much reflection by Francione, concerns a case—certainly marginal—of human-nonhuman interaction, which obliges us to compare the mutual rights or, at least, the level at which they should be placed according to the philosophy abolitionist. As many have questioned whether the attribution of rights to animals can determine even a reversal of the relationship, what should a castaway, lost on a desert island without plants do? Should he starve, or would he be justified if he decided to eat fish or birds to survive? Francione replied: "*Eating a nonhuman—or another human—might be excusable in such circumstances.*" The reference of the philosopher is, in this case, the equal consideration of the interests, and the response shows how, in his thinking, it is not possible to draw any superiority even in favor of animals, but an equal appreciation of all needs.

One criticism that is often given to those who adopt the vegan diet is that it would be inconsistent to feed pets with food produced through the exploitation and killing of other animals.

Some vegans face the issue in one way, others the other way. There are those who refuse to feed carnivorous or omnivorous animals such as cats and dogs in a manner deemed unnatural, but there are some who choose to boycott the retail of animal food at all costs; the latter are often accused of immorality, for having unduly interfered with the nature of pets, altering.

What solution would be more in line with morality? "*Our dogs have been vegans for decades and have done very well. Some cats can't. As I have argued, that is a problem of domestication that should be abolished anyway. In any event, I argue feeding meat to cats who will die if they don't get it as falling into the 'excusable' category.*"

A particular question concerns the object of this work, namely the establishment of a special law that provides the right of vegetarians/vegans to find alternative menus at restaurants. What prospects could have a similar law? Would it be useful? According to Francione *"laws will be useless until there is a critical mass of vegans."*

Francione's answer reflects the thoughts expressed about the possibility of a transition period; all the instruments adopted in the transitional period should in fact contribute to the affirmation of a coherent thought in society and push, therefore, through the instruments of political and economic pressure, the final change.

One of the tools that some may allow to abandon the exploitation of animals would be the in vitro meat, which is the kind of meat synthetically produced in a laboratory.

Some argue that this is an unfounded assumption, since there are already some vegetable alternatives to meat.

Professor Francione says he does not share the optimism that some have expressed about in vitro meat and declares: *"I think that in vitro meat is a silly concept. It will be too expensive, and those who really want the meat won't be happy with it."*

1.5 BEKOFF-PIERCE AND MORALS
IN NONHUMAN ANIMALS' SOCIETIES

Morality, Justice, and Method

Many thinkers of all ages have discussed the meaning of terms such as "morality" and "justice," and everyone sees different meanings and implications, thus arriving at mixed results.

If it is not easy to define certain concepts in the context of society and human relationships, it is even more complex in the case of nonhuman subjects, or interactions between different species.

One of the clichés of philosophy, or at least the predominant philosophical currents, is that morality is an exclusive attribution of human beings and that, therefore, nonhumans are radically excluded from moral acts or sense.

Some philosophers—Regan and Francione included—decided to extend the moral theory to also include nonhumans, or at least some of them (as the subjects-of-a-life); in doing so, we have also used scientific instruments, such as observations from the natural sciences about the possibility that nonhumans are sentient.

Francione and Regan, with arguments and conclusions sometimes different, have derived from the sentient nature of animals their position as moral patients; in doing so, there has not been recognized to them the ability to act according to a moral system, but merely a general duty of inclusion in human moral theories.

Conceptually, one can distinguish a gradation among skills that philosophy has recognized to nonhumans:

1. *Cartesian mechanism;*
2. *sentience (Bentham and utilitarianism);*
3. *behaviors and attitudes or pseudo proto human (Regan, Francione).*

The last frontier, so far unsurpassed, is now approached by science, which seeks to dissolve a question that many did not dare to discuss: can nonhumans act on the basis of morality or justice?

Marc Bekoff, a scientist, along with Jessica Pierce, a philosopher, tried to provide an answer that, unlike the philosophical hypotheses, should be based only on empirical data.

Since it is impossible to discuss morality without taking into account the underlying philosophical issues and that they must necessarily be related to the observation, from this joint effort, the two authors have derived the book *Wild Justice.*[107]

The first question that the authors try to answer is: *what does it mean to act morally?*

First of all, an action based on the moral sense is not necessarily a right or correct action, and, therefore, they exclude that attributing moral capacity to a subject implies a positive or negative conduct.

The authors take as the definition of morality *"set of behaviors related and directed towards others, intended to develop and govern complex interactions within social groups. These behaviors are related to welfare and suffering; in addition, many of these are applicable criteria of right and wrong."*[108]

Subjects of research and analysis are, in particular, three types of behavior:

* *Cooperation;*
* *Empathy;*
* *Justice.*

In the first pattern are included behaviors such as altruism, reciprocity, trust, punishment, and revenge, while in the second there are empathy, compassion, sorrow, consolation, etc. In the pattern of justice behaviors such as honesty, sharing, expectations about what you believe you deserve, punishment, resentment, etc. are taken into account.

All three patterns in question would be united by the necessary elements of moral qualities, while the last one, in particular, has a significance all of its own, as it would allow one to ascertain that neither the concept of morality, nor that of justice are exclusive to the human species.

Which species may be capable of moral behavior?

The common opinion, that even the most prominent advocates of animal rights philosophers, such as Tom Regan, have been shown to share, is that the mind of those animals most biologically similar to the human species are also similar to those of the human species.

If it is true that human beings evolved from primates and share with them the greater part of the heritage, it is more instinctive to also consider primates mentally and emotionally more similar; the same argument could relate to particular animals, whose behaviors are best known and comprehensible to humans due to cohabitation: many living with cats or dogs are more prone to humanize them and, therefore, to recognize in their behavior characteristics that are similar to their own.

The study of Bekoff and Pierce denies one of the most deeply rooted clichés on the capabilities of the minds of nonhumans: the moral conduct would not only be characteristic of primates, cats and dogs or horses, but of animals of any kind, including rats and cetaceans.

The absence of studies on many species prevents comments on their moral skills and, for this reason, the list must necessarily be left open pending further investigation.

Scientific analysis would seem to disprove the theory of the subjects-of-a-life, confined to mammals' qualifications as moral subjects:

> It is possible that morality is an exclusive feature of mammals, around which the book is centered. However, at the point where we are, it would be premature to declare that other species do not have them. The fact is that we simply lack sufficient data to incontrovertible statements on how cognitive and emotional skills necessary to feel empathy, decency, or morality act are taxonomically distributed. We must therefore suspend judgment. For example, it is conceivable that some birds, such as corvids, which include species remarkably intelligent, have a certain kind of morality [109]

Also, the studies carried out on relationships within insect societies suggest data compatible with encoded behaviors that normally characterize moral actions, and these behaviors are defined by the authors as "prosocial" and are distinct from those morals, since only the latter possess

> a certain degree of complexity in social organization, including behavioral norms established which reconnect strong emotional and cognitive stimulations about what is right or wrong, a certain level of complexity of the nervous system that serves as the basis for emotional and for decision-making based on a sense of the past and the future; sufficiently advanced cognitive abilities (a good memory, for example), a high level of behavioral flexibility [110]

The basis of morality would be intelligence and sociability: these two elements combined would result in that evolutionary adaptation that can be defined as "morality."

The concept of justice is in close connection with sociality and morality, which Bekoff and Pierce try to describe, starting from the definition provided by the Merriam-Webster Dictionary of English: *"Right: what is deserved or be worthy to receive. Justice: t he maintenance or administration of what is just especially by the impartial adjustment of conflicting claims or the assignment of merited rewards or punishments."*[111]

Synthesizing the dictionary definition, the authors define what they mean as right in the book: *"A set of expectations about what you are worthy to receive and how you should be treated."*[112]

Bekoff and Pierce's thesis is that the idea of justice is innate in man, and that it manifests an evolutionary continuity that would make it impossible to exclude nonhumans from the list of those who possess it, and, of course, the concept of justice that Bekoff and Pierce take into account is not that of the legal human, as the perception of individuals to deserve or not deserve something.

Another indication that the sense of justice has not been acquired (being innate) is apparent in the behavior of children, who would be able to demonstrate this feature within a few months of age; for example, preferring the characters that play the role of "good" in a representation of puppets.[113]

The ability to develop a sense of morality or justice would be one of the countless adaptations, since, in fact, it represents the foundation of the community and a necessary element for their survival in the long-term; the confirmation of this would be to recognize the fact that the majority of moral behaviors observed in nonhumans manifest cooperation rather than competition.

The object of the study has a number of controversial issues, which the authors do not fail to point out, taking into account the main criticisms against their theories:

- animals are not smart enough to have morality;
- do not have emotions;
- cannot empathize;
- are not rational;
- lack reflective judgment;
- are not moral agents;
- lack conscience.

The first four, according to the authors, are easily overcome through the observation and study of animal behavior, both in the wild and in captivity, or in coexistence with man—the denial of these prerogatives is therefore exclusively the result of an incorrect knowledge of the matter.

More controversial is the possibility that nonhumans lack reflective judgment, but Bekoff and Pierce argue that it would be wrong to infer that the absence of this skill also implies the absence of moral behavior; there is no evidence that the reflective judgment is a necessary precondition of morality.

The last two criticisms are more complex, as they have different interpretations. The definition of morality has been interpreted by philosophy in many ways—according to the authors, it is possible that all the known definitions are wrong.

According to some scientists, indeed, it would be incorrect to attribute only to the authority of philosophers' discourse in matters of morality, since the role of biology in the matter would be prevalent; it is a hypothesis that Bekoff and Pierce do not share, highlighting the complexity of the concept of morality.

The ability to act independently is, without a doubt, necessary for an entity to be considered capable of morally oriented actions; excluding the possibility that animals are guided only by instinct, it must be concluded that they have the ability to distinguish their actions on the basis of morality.

Then there is the controversial issue of consciousness, which by many philosophers has been considered a dividing line for the attribution of moral capacities; about it, as well as on the moral, the authors suggest two questions:

- *Is consciousness a precondition for morality?*
- *Do animals have consciousness?*

According to Darwin, each animal with well-marked social instincts would be able to develop a conscience. He noted the ability of self-control in particular, which they have, pointing out that their behavior was the result of a conflict between opposed impulses, which showed the awareness of the existence of a choice.[114]

Darwin's statement implies further study: Can we consider that the power of self-control by itself is equivalent to consciousness? Can it be argued that the ability to control the instinct is sufficient to recognize a moral behavior?

The conclusion of the authors in relation to the criticism that, by denying the consciousness of animals, one rejects their moral capacities, is that even showing that they will not have that skill, it will not be possible to automatically say that they are not capable of moral behavior.

Normally the possession of consciousness has been used as an argument to distinguish human animals from all others, considering that a qualitative difference.

According to Bekoff and Pierce, the traditional approach should be revised; any difference connected with the presence or not of consciousness, would be only quantitative.[115]

Morality in Nonhuman Societies

The relevance of moral duties has been widely highlighted by philosophers of all time, so much so that its first manifestation consists in the formulation of the category of duties, while that of rights is only later, and consequential.

Prohibitions are a known category, also present in nonhuman societies; they are connected with behaviors that the individual has with others and that can lead to a benefit or a detriment.

Typical examples of duties in nonhuman societies are the rules that require one to repay advantageous actions received or to help those in need, but also adhere to the hierarchies, putting individuals on different statuses.

The "animal morality," the authors warn, is a general concept, which defines a heterogeneous phenomenon; in fact, it is not possible to define just one moral valid for all species, but each species or group adopts different rules of behavior and different penalties.

To better explain the concept, Bekoff and Pierce argue that the variability of morality is also a known fact within human societies: historical, cultural, and geographic have different moral systems that sometimes produce the opposite. A similar argument applies to the community of nonhumans, which, to a human observer, often appear to be free of moral qualities because of the remoteness of the principles adopted and events.

The social complexity of human communities is unique and, at the same time, at a maximum level; the use of symbolic language has made it possible to add elements that deeply characterize the relationship, impossible to find in nonhumans.

As opposed to moral behavior, or at least morally positive, there are those behaviors considered immoral and that the authors identify as the ones that go *"against society's expectations."*[116] In this sense, it could not be possible to attribute any kind of moral implication to the action of a wolf killing a deer to eat, since between those two animals there are not social conventions of any kind and there is no system of reciprocity.

Preliminary thoughts dispelled the doubts and clarified the fundamental differences; it is possible to understand, without bias, the variety of moral behaviors of nonhuman species, of which the authors provide some clarifying examples.

In 1996, the news reported that a three-year-old child had fallen into the gorilla enclosure in the zoo in Brookfield (Illinois). He was picked up and cradled by a female gorilla, who had then brought him up to the door, to deliver him into the hands of the zoo staff.[117]

The behavior of the female gorilla has been widely analyzed and provides an index of the capacity for empathy, compassion, and altruism that so far have been almost unanimously attributed to humans exclusively.

Empathy describes a series of behaviors attributable to different levels, which can be schematically indicated as so:

1. *physiological reflex;*
2. *emotional empathy;*
3. *cognitive empathy.*

The first-level answers are essentially connected with automatic imitations of others' movements, which do not require complex or abstract mental abilities.

The emotional empathy requires the ability to provide targeted support.

The cognitive empathy represents the level of maximum advance, in which the individual is able not only to feel another's emotions, but also to understand the reasons behind them and, therefore, regulate his actions.[118]

Recent studies on nerve cells have determined the existence of "mirror neurons," namely neurons whose function would be to enable understanding of others' behaviors, allowing an individual to carry out a process of identification.[119]

The research on mirror neurons is only beginning, but it has already allowed us to identify their existence in nonhuman animals such as rats and birds.[120] This discovery would provide the biological explanation of behaviors that have already been observed for many decades. An example is that of the rat who, if it can feed only by causing a shock to his fellow rat, desists from doing so; it is a behavior that does not presuppose any interest or advantage, either direct or indirect, and that, on the contrary, causes a disadvantage to the acting subject.

Another kind of neurons involved in empathetic and intuitive proceedings is that of "fusiform," whose presence in cetaceans is approximately three times that of the human brain.[121]

The ability to empathize was also considered the essential tool of the utilitarian morality by Hare, because it makes the agent aware of the implications of his actions and, therefore, of the interests of others involved.

The axiom of Hare could be summarized as follows: those who are not capable of feeling pain are not able to recognize such in the other.

Another example of "unexpected" empathy between animals reported by the authors was of two mice, unable to get out of a sink, trudging till they are exhausted, and when one received a container with water, since the other is too tired to get there, the first recovers a piece of food, tenders it to the other, and moves ever closer to the water, until the first gets to drink.[122] Behaviors that assume certain responsibilities, which were often considered exclusive of humans, were observed in many animals. Among these were "mutualism" and "reciprocal altruism."

The mutualism consists of an exchange between individuals based on a contextual give and receive; animals such as lions or wolves, for example, hunt in this way.

In mutualism all individuals involved derive an immediate benefit, and in particular circumstances, such as hunting, the result is greater efficiency compared to the individual action.

Reciprocal altruism, even more than mutualism, challenges the more radicated ideas in respect to nonhumans' mental faculties and, in particular, will shed new light on one of the most controversial aspects of contemporary philosophy: the sense of time.

While the mutualism, with the immediacy of the benefit that distinguishes it, does not imply abstractive attitudes, it can be concluded the opposite for the conduct that aims to the future and hypothetical benefit, which characterizes reciprocal altruism.

In the utilitarian perspective, the ability to prefigure the future has been considered a fundamental discriminant with respect to the interest for the continuation of life: being aware of time passing also allows one to accrue up to expectations and, therefore, frustrate them by interrupting the existence.

Grooming is an example of known reciprocal altruism. It is a social practice that, based on the removal of parasites from the body (from fur), consists of the handling and in the contact that takes place on the basis of precise rules.

The one who received grooming will pay it back to the individual who delivered it, and arrangements will be similar, especially duration; this observation suggests the possession of abstractive faculty and maturation of expectations toward the future.

This kind of complex behaviors, which are conventionally believed to be an attribution exclusive of humans and, at most, of the most developed of primates, has been reported in many different species, even ones far different from humans.

Vampire bats feed on the blood of other animals and, in doing so, they share food with individuals unable to procure it themselves, benefiting mostly those who have done so for them in the past; this would be a case of reciprocal altruism. [123]

The thesis of the authors is that a greater intellectual and social development may correspond to more complex moral behavior, even if it is not possible to determine precisely which species can be considered to have at least three elements that characterize the prerequisites of morally oriented behavior at the present time.

Bekoff and Pierce provide an example of increased complexity in moral behavior, from the study of the anthropologist Barbara J. King on a chimpanzee, Tina, who lived in a community of chimpanzees and was killed by a leopard. The group's dominant male kept watching Tina's body for five hours, avoiding any contact or interference and rejecting all other chimpanzees, except one: her brother.

As the authors argue the dominant male recognized the emotional bond between brother and sister, and, therefore, allowed him – and just him, nobody else – to approach her body.

On the other hand Tarzan, Tina's brother, showed strong emotions, sitting close to Tina's body and touching it [124] .

Through the analysis of a large case series, the authors conclude that many nonhuman behaviors, both toward their own kind rather than individuals of other species, would be morally oriented and that, therefore, it would not be appropriate to continue to believe that only humans are capable of expressing moral evaluations.

Justice in Nonhuman Societies

Is it possible that nonhuman animals know or even practice justice?

At a simple level, the question can be answered by returning to some of the main philosophical currents; the natural law may well lead to an affirmative answer, while, according to legal positivism, believing that there can be no justice outside of rules enacted by the law, the amenability of this concept to any nonhuman species should be excluded.

At the base of the diverse currents of thought, there is a different definition of justice; it can be considered abstract and absolute, or relative and concrete, as well as pre-existing humans or having been invented by them.

The question that, perhaps more than any other, has divided philosophers in the field of justice is if humans, making law, just detect and codify something that pre-exists, or if they create something new.

Bobbio, in stating that the foundation of right lies in the consent of associates, excluded any absolute nature, putting maximum importance on the human will and the social and cultural forces that, in turn, bring it to life.

Contractualists, considering the origin law in covenants, excluded animals, as they are unable to join (or comply with) any covenant.

The feature that has united thinkers who have approached the problem of justice referring to nonhumans is that the latter have always been taken into account in their relationship with humans, so then, not from an absolute, but relative, perspective.

Many believe that granting rights to animals shall be possible only once demonstrated that they are sentient or morally relevant subjects.

It is probably not a coincidence that the naturalist de Waal has observed that: "*Reading* A Theory of Justice *, the influential work of the contemporary philosopher John Rawls, I cannot escape the feeling that instead of describ-*

ing human innovation, he develops ancient themes, many of whom are recognizable in our closest relatives."[125] ."

Bekoff and Pierce, starting from the study of morality, seem to go beyond, exploring a place little or never practiced, such as the existence of a system of justice, apart from the human one, where animals join in a manner not dissimilar to humans.

Of course, it is the concept of justice that the authors have initially defined and described as maturation of expectations on the part of individuals about what they consider whether or not to deserve and as their reaction to the frustration of those expectations. An example to clarify the concept comes from the same Bekoff and Pierce: "*Sergio Pellis has found that rats, during a play sequence, control each other, adapting behavior to maintain the atmosphere of the game. When there is no compliance with the rules, they will also stop the playful interaction, which, therefore, even in rats, revolves around fairness and trust.*"[126]

The authors point out the different attitude of different species to develop expectations toward other individuals, warning of the risk of confusing the human system with that of nonhumans.

A 2007 study conducted by Keith Jensen at the Max Planck Institute is used as an example of the risk of misunderstanding the real meaning of human behaviors without abandoning the cultural conditioning of its context. Some chimpanzees were offered raisins to share with a fellow; all individuals had retained the greatest amount of food, leaving the bottom to the partner, but none of them had complained for not having received exactly half.[127]

The conclusion of the research is that the human sense of justice is an exclusive, that not even apes share; if this were not, in fact, the case they would have protested for a fair division of food.

Bekoff and Pierce disagree with Jensen's conclusions, stating that he did not considered the differences between our and their sense of moral, and that – therefore – stating that chimpanzees lack any sense of justice is, at least, imprudent[128] .

What emerges from the discussion of the two authors is that even the definition of the concept of justice is far from unequivocal and can take on nuances sometimes at odds.

Bekoff and Pierce consider particularly relevant the game, as a fundamental expression of the logic of nonhumans expectations and punishments; such volunteer activity is based on shared rules, the transgression of which entails the imposition of actual sanctions.

Two dogs playing, in the authors' example, accept each other's limitations, adapting to the rules governing the game: the strength of bites, the prohibition to mate, limit or avoid dominance.

In the game between dogs we see ritualized movements, positions, and behavior, which reflects the set of rules that allows individuals who participate to understand the purpose and intentions of others involved.

If one of the participants in the game violates the rules, such as biting too hard, another undergoes a first sanction, which could be called a "recall," namely a moderate reaction of condemnation of his behavior through vocalizations or a physical response accentuated.

In the event that the violation is repeated, the subject undergoes a more severe sanction, which tends to result in exclusion from the game. This measure may be temporary or lasting, but, in general, individuals who do not respect the rules of the game are ousted by the community. [129]

The concept of justice found in animals at play is based on the expectation: each feels the "right" behavior, what is expected from the other, and when such expectation is disregarded, it is shown disapproval and the partner is punished accordingly.

> In Ultimately, it may be that the game represents a unique behavioral category, since the asymmetries are much more tolerated than in other social contexts. Pets are committed to really reduce the disparities in body size, strength, social status, and to achieve the same involvement. The game cannot take place if individuals choose not to be involved and in the need to be based on fairness on both sides so that it can continue makes, it is different from other forms of cooperative behavior (such as hunting). This activity is based on a form of egalitarianism that is perhaps unique. If justice is defined as a set of rules of social expectations that neutralize individual differences in order to maintain the harmony of the group, then it is precisely what is found in animals when they play. [130]

The sense of justice affected by the frustration of social expectations can be fulfilled also by the "apology" of the offender, which in the case of dogs is manifested through the "bow," a particular body posture assumed and maintained in a conventional way.

The bow is also used to anticipate and explain their intentions, so there are no misunderstandings and, for example, the desire to play will not be confused with aggression.

The game has been observed in many species; in particular, Bekoff and Pierce emphasize that there would be correspondence between those able to practice and those that expressed moral attitudes.

In the playful context, the authors see also the affirmation of the principle of equality, since all individuals involved operate on an equal level, even giving up the benefits of their social status and dominance. The role reversal and self-restraint assume a fundamental importance in this context.

A dominant male who agrees to play with another voluntarily waives the right to exercise his supremacy and, for example, can submit and limit his strength to match that of counterparts; not doing so would result in him being ousted from the social practice of the game. [131]

Individuals who do not participate in the games of their fellows end up being marginalized and spend most of the time in solitude; that, in nature, implies a greater likelihood that the individual leaves the group and that, consequently, leading a solitary life, is about three times more exposed to the dangers and an early death. [132]

Bekoff and Pierce see remarkable similarities between animals' social behavior in gaming and that of human beings, stating that a higher risk of developing heart diseases is connected with the human sense of injustice: those bad feelings possibly affect some body's processes as direct consequences. [133]

Outside of the game, in general, the manifestation of the sense of justice in relation to the distribution of resources can be approached from two different perspectives:

* *Indignation at having received less than one fellow;*
* *Indignation at having received more than one fellow.*

> Brosnan first trained a group of capuchins to use small pieces of rock as tokens of exchange for food. Pairs of females were asked to swap a piece of granite for a grape. A second monkey, who had just witnessed the rock-for-grape trade, was asked to swap a rock for a piece of cucumber, a much less desirable treat. The short-changed monkey would refuse to cooperate with the researchers and wouldn't eat the cucumber and often threw it back at the human. In a nutshell, the capuchins expected to be treated fairly. They seemed to measure and compare rewards in relation to those around them. A single monky who traded a rock for a cucumber would be delighted with the outcome. It was only when others seemed to get something better that the cucumber suddenly became undesireable [134] .

The feeling of justice would be an essential element of a community, both human and nonhuman, and would also serve as a benchmark of selfishness. A society based on individuals who do not meet the expectations of others, trying to cater exclusively to their own, would be devoid of trust, which is an essential requirement of cohabitation.

Just as in the game, in all other social relations, lack of confidence determines shyness and social exclusion, limiting or precluding the links and making it impossible to have collaboration and cooperation. From this point of view, the fact that they have a sense of justice would represent yet another evolution shared by humans and nonhumans.

On the issue of justice, Bekoff and Pierce conclude that:

Human morality is unique. In human societies, the ability to decide abstractly who deserves what and why is of vital importance. We could consider human innovation, specialization, a refinement of the ability to be fair. It can be said that justice, as expressed in human societies, is both more complex and more nuanced than in other animal societies. But that does not in any way mean to argue that animals cannot have it. [135]

Conclusions on Animals' Morality

Is it possible to include nonhumans in the group of moral agents?

We like to say that this step is neither too long nor particularly difficult. In philosophical language, a moral agent is one who freely chooses to act in one way rather than another, and is responsible for his own actions. Being moral agents is generally opposed to being moral patients and such distinction between patients and agents is used to mark a distinction between those able to make moral choices and those who are unable [...]. This dichotomy between agents and patients, although useful in limited contexts, may also be misleading.

Arguing that animals have a capacity to act morally does not mean to argue the equality with similar human condition. [136]

At the conclusion of the work, Bekoff and Pierce, aware of the path to be explored and the need to deepen not only the information on the matter, but also their implications, say that it can currently be concluded that *"animals have a kind of moral intelligence."* [137]

De Waal, repeatedly cited by the authors, came to similar conclusions but was more cautious, merely recognizing in nonhuman primates the possibility to *"experience the first signs of human morality."* [138]

How can we place the research of Bekoff and Pierce, about moral issues in relation to different species? In a contractualist perspective, the fact that nonhumans cannot manifest moral attitudes is irrelevant, as is the fact that, in their company, they are able to follow certain rules, and possibly respect a sort of social contract. In this context, it should be asked whether animals have demonstrated the ability to enter into a social contract with the men, but that fact seems to be discarded, even by the authors.

Utilitarianism and deontologism, based on the attitude of empathy and moral individuals, will be able to find important arguments in Bekoff and Pierce's work, especially with regard to empathy. In fact, several examples are given that support the presence of such capacity in nonhumans.

Whether animals are or are not able to implement forms of justice seems irrelevant, not making, by itself, any additional argument to Singer, Regan, and Francione's theories.

NOTES

1. Pisanò, *Diritti deumanizzati. Animali, ambiente, generazioni future, specie umana*, Giuffrè, Milano, 2012.
2. Bobbio, *L'età dei diritti*, Einaudi, Torino, 1990.
3. Ibid., p. 7.
4. Ibid.
5. Ibid., p. 15.
6. Ibid., p. 16.
7. Ibid., p. 52.
8. Ibid., p. 52.
9. Locke, John, *Second Treatise of Government*, Hackett Publishing Company, 1980.
10. B obbio, *Diritti dell'uomo e società*, in " *Sociologia del diritto* ", 1989, n. 1, p. 25.
11. Ibid.., p. 68.
12. Ibid.., p. 75.
13. Ibid., p. 81.
14. ———, *Destra e sinistra*, Donzelli, Roma, 1994, p. 120.
15. Ignatieff, Michael, *Human Right as Politics and Idolatry*, Princeton University Press, 2001, pp. 24-25.
16. Ibid., p. 124.
17. Ibid., p. 58.
18. Ibid., p. 91.
19. Ferrajoli, Vitale, *Diritti fondamentali. Un dibattito teorico*, Roma-Bari, Laterza, I ed., 2001, p. 5.
20. Ferrajoli, *Dai diritti del cittadino ai diritti della persona*, in Zolo, D., *La cittadinanza. Appartenenza, identità, diritti*, Roma-Bari, Laterza, 1999, p. 288.
21. Pisanò, p. 9.
22. Ibid., p. 10.
23. Ibid., p. 11.
24. Ryder, R.D., *Victims of Science. The Use of Animals in Research*, London, Davis-Poynter, 1975.
25. Varner, op. cit., p. 240.
26. Pisanò, op. cit., p. 15.
27. Ibid., p. 21.
28. Ibid., p. 23.
29. Ibid., p. 24.
30. Lodovici, G.S., *L'utilità del bene. Jeremy Bentham, l'utilitarismo e il consequenzialismo*, Vita e Pensiero, Milano, 2004, p. 10.
31. Bhikhu C. Parekh, *Jeremy Bentham, Critical Assessments*, Routledge, UK, 1993, p. 66.
32. Bentham, Jeremy, *An Introduction to the Principles of Morals and Legislation* [1780], Dover, 2007, New York, USA, p. 311.
33. Varner, Gary E., Personhood, *Ethics, and Animal Cognition: Situating Animals in Hare's Two-Level Utilitarianism*, Oxford University Press, 2012, p. 159.
34. Singer, *Practical Ethics*, Cambridge University Press, 1979, p. 75.
35. Varner, p. 186, 218.
36. Varner, p. 229.
37. Varner, p. 240.
38. Singer, *Animal Liberation*, Harper Collins, 1975, p.170.
39. Ibid.
40. Ibid., p. 228.
41. Singer, *Rethinking Life and Death*, St. Martin's Press, 1996, p. 194.
42. Ibid.
43. Hengelardt, *The Foundations of Bioethics*, 2nd edition, Oxford University Press, 1996.
44. Spaemann, *Persons*, Oxford University Press, 2006, p. 232.
45. Varner, p. 228.
46. Bhikhu, p. 61.

47. Singer, *Practical Ethics*, p. 57.
48. Ibid.
49. Singer, *Animal Liberation*, p. 18.
50. Mason, Jim, Singer, Peter, *The Ethics of What We Eat*, Rodale, USA, 2006.
51. Ibid., p. 3.
52. Ibid., p. 250.
53. Kant, *Groundworks of the Metaphysics of Morals*, 2nd edition, Cambridge University Press, 2012, p. 66.
54. ———, *Dei doveri verso gli animali e gli spiriti*, in *Lezioni di etica*, Laterza, Bari, 1971, p. 273.
55. Ibid.
56. Regan, *The Case for Animal Rights*, University of California Press, 1983, pp. 253-254.
57. Rawls, *A Theory of Justice*, Oxford University Press, 1971, p. 418.
58. Ibid.
59. Regan, *The Case for Animal Rights*, p. 214.
60. Ibid., p. 215.
61. Ibid., p. 56.
62. Descartes, *Discourse on the Method*, SMK Books, 2009.
63. Regan, *The Case for Animal Rights*, p. 44.
64. Ibid., p. 286.
65. Ibid., p. 291.
66. Singer, *Practical Ethics*, p. 24.
67. Regan, *The Case for Animal Rights*, p. 308.
68. Ibid., p. 331.
69. Ibid., p. 124.
70. Ibid., p. 327.
71. Ibid., p. 331.
72. Ibid., p. 354.
73. Ibid., p. 385.
74. Ibid., p. 382.
75. Ibid., p. 414.
76. Ibid., p. 422.
77. Ibid., p. 462.
78. Ibid., p. 472.
79. Ibid., p. 447.
80. Ibid., p. 451.
81. Ibid., p. 451.
82. Ibid., p. 453.
83. Ibid., p. 460.
84. Ibid., p. 464.
85. http://law.newark.rutgers.edu/our-faculty/faculty-profiles/gary-l-francione
86. https://www.facebook.com/abolitionistapproach
87. http://www.abolitionistapproach.com/
88. Francione, Gary, *Animals as Persons: Essays on the Abolition of Animal Exploitation*, Columbia University Press, New York, 2008, foreword by Gary Steiner.
89. Ibid., acknowledgments.
90. Ibid., p. 13.
91. Regan, *The Case for Animal Rights*, p. 324.
92. Singer, *Ten Years of Animal Liberation*, New York Review of Books, January 17, 1985, p. 49.
93. ———, *Animals, Property and the Law*, Temple University Press, Philadelphia, 1995, p. 51.
94. Francione, *Animals as Persons*, p. 161.
95. Sunstein, *Slaughterhouse Jive*, New Republic at 44.
96. Francione, *Animals as Persons*, p. 231.
97. ———, *Animals, Property, and The Law*, p. 67.

98. ———, *Animals as Persons*, p. 167.
99. Ibid., p. 227.
100. ———, *Introduction to Animal Rights: Your Child or the Dog?*, Temple University Press, Philadelphia, 2000, p. 153.
101. ———, *Animals as Persons*, p. 188.
102. Ibid.
103. Ibid., p. 109.
104. Ibid.
105. Ibid., p. 107.
106. ———, *Animals, Property, and the Law*, p. 260.
107. Bekoff, Pierce, *Wild Justice,* University of Chicago Press, 2009.
108. Ibid., p. 32.
109. Ibid., p. 35.
110. Ibid., p. 40.
111. Ibid., p. 171.
112. Ibid., p. 63.
113. Ibid., p. 172.
114. Ibid., p. 215.
115. Ibid., p. 217.
116. Ibid., p. 45.
117. Ibid., p. 24.
118. Ibid., p. 139.
119. Ibid., p. 60.
120. Ibid., p. 61.
121. Ibid., p. 62.
122. Ibid., p. 134.
123. Ibid., p. 120.
124. King, B. J., in *Primatology.net*, 31 gennaio 2007, http://primatology.net/2007/01/31/on-god-gorillas-and-theevolution-of-religion, citato in Bekoff, Pierce, op cit., p. 151.
125. De Waal, Franz, Good Natured*: The Origins of Right and Wrong in Humans and Other Animals*, Harvard University Press, 1997, p. 161.
126. Bekoff, Pierce, p. 186.
127. Gellene, D., *Fairness Is Only Human, Scientist Find*, in *Los Angeles Times*, October, 5th, 2007, in Bekoff, Pierce, p. 167.
128. Bekoff, Pierce, p. 168.
129. Ibid., p. 176.
130. Ibid., p. 182.
131. Ibid., p. 185.
132. Ibid., p. 193.
133. Ibid., p. 194.
134. Ibid., p. 190.
135. Ibid., p. 197.
136. Ibid., p. 214.
137. Ibid., p. 225.
138. Ibid., p. 35.

Chapter Two

The Legal Framework of Relations between Human and Nonhuman Animals

The Conceptual Framework of Animals in Greek and Roman Law

The tradition of Western law, in relation to animals, has its roots in Greek and Roman ones. Even the ancient Greeks distinguished between the law of men (δίκη) and of animals (νόμος), explaining that, while men are subject to the laws of civil society, animals are ruled by the law of nature, based on the instincts and the prevalence of the fittest. [1]

The Roman era is dominated by the bifurcation of Ulpian, who had distinguished between *ius naturae* and *ius gentium*[2] , stating that: "*Ius naturale est, quod natura omnia animali docuit.*"[3]

The law of nature, as innate and absolute, governs the lives and relationships of all animals, while the right of the people, as human creation, would be exclusive of the human species.

The most interesting feature of the classical concept of *ius naturae* is the conceptual identification of humans with nonhumans, which, suggesting the membership of all to the same context, also considers them subject to the same laws. In this feature we observe the difference from the Greek tradition, which had formulated in an organic way a conceptual distinction between humans and nonhumans, attributing it to divine will.

Roman law does not deal in any way to protect the interests of nonhuman animals, but devotes several rules to the latter; the common feature of all Roman laws is the classification of animals as *res*.

The reason for the equalization of nonhumans to things is not philosophical, but eminently practical; their use by humans, especially with reference to the underlying economic implications, presupposed the adoption of legislation relating to the ownership and responsibility equivalent to that of any other moving object, subject to the peculiarities of the case. [4]

The fundamental distinction between animals in Roman law is among those owned by someone (human), and those that are not (or are no longer): i.e. those not domesticated, not belonging to other humans, were considered *res nullius* (or *res derelictae*) and, as such, freely available for anyone. [5]

Pulling and pack animals were considered *res mancipi*[6] , that is, they were essential for an economy based on agriculture and livestock; the ox, in particular, was considered *socius* of humans, who used it for plowing the field.s[7]

The Roman law, while not acknowledging any legal subjectivity to nonhumans, however, provided peculiar institutions, recognizing substantial differences from the category of *res* and placing them in a state of conceptual conflict, such as "objects" with will and self-determination.

We must give account that even the nonhuman animals qualification in Roman law is not uncontroversial, since some argue that such a condition was due entirely the same of *res*, and who, conversely, argues that the modern conceptual distinction was unknown to the Romans and the categories were less rigid and absolute. For example, the human being itself could be considered a person or thing, depending on whether it was free or a slave. [8]

The *animus revertendi* is a prerogative given to pets (or domesticated animals), recognized by the Roman law in order to ensure the economic value and safeguard the interests of owners: taking note of their propensity to return from the master, it was recognized legal significance to such behavior, preventing the animals that had manifested it from being considered *res derelictae*.

Actions for Damages for the Harm Caused by Animals

The Roman legislator took into consideration two main types of questions related to animals: the damage caused *by* these and the damage caused *to* them. [9]

A particularly important legal institution, belonging to the first category, is *actio de pauperie*, a special occupation that included the obligation to compensate the owner of animals if they had caused unpredictable damage. [10]

The *actio de pauperie* is a noxal action and, therefore, it is applied the rule "*noxa caput sequitur,*" attesting a real recognition of subjectivity in relation to nonhumans, so that the liability for damages is not of the owner at the time of the damage, but of whoever owned the animal at the time of the request.[11]

The action for the depletion[12] is not intended as punishment for the owner's conduct, but it depends on the animal's conduct; in case of death or sale of the same, the owner is no longer liable to pay any compensation.

It is also interesting to note that in the *Actio de pauperie* there is a distinction between natural and unnatural behaviors of animals; the responsibility for imponderable actions are exerted on the owners and, in fact, it has objective in nature, finding its limit in the accident.[13]

Another legal institution relating to cases of damage caused by animals is the *Actio de pastu pecoris*. In this case, nonhumans are considered equivalent to objects and the responsibility falls entirely on the owner, who illegally entered cattle into someone else's field, feeding them.[14]

The *Actio de pastu pecoris* regards a particular and limited case. In the first place, it was not attributable to the behavior of any animal, but only to that of the so-called *pecudes*[15] ; moreover, it did not relate to malicious behavior in general, but only to those which result in misuse of others' food resources.

Much more general is the scope of the *Lex Aquilia de damno*, which covers all cases of damage caused by the behavior of any pet, due to the owner's responsibility.

If the *Actio de pauperie* emphasized the distinction between nonhuman animals and a mere *res*, the *Actio aquiliana* completely equalizes things and animals, indiscriminately punishing the owner of the one and the other.

The dividing line between the two institutions is subtle and sometimes depends on the opinion of the judge, who must determine the etiology of animal behavior, noting whether it was or was not conformable to nature, or if it was caused by the owner.[16]

Certainly, the domestic dog is not included in the *pecudes*, being part of the *quadrupes* category, though even in their respect, there are actions existing that require compensation for damage caused by the responsibility of the owner or by *contra naturam* behaviors.

The Edictum de Feris

Animals that are not the property of any human being are considered *res nullius*, therefore extraneous to the liability regime established with the abovementioned *actiones*, which implies the amenability of the first to an owner, so that this one could be liable for damages.

The relationship between humans and nonhumans in Roman society is essentially based on three guiding principles: use for economic purposes, companionship, and entertainment. The first two reports, in the case of damage to a third party, are disciplined in the abovesaid institutions, while the third case is of greater complexity.

"Amusement" animals in the *Urbe* were wild, imported from distant regions in the course of military campaigns. To use them in the circus performances they had to be transported within the city, thus exposing people and properties to the risk of damage during transportation and travel.

To face the risk of the introduction of wild animals in urban environments, *curule aediles* had issued the *Edictum de feris*[17] , stating the obligation to make reparation for any damage caused during wild animals' transportation.

The list of species included in the edict was mandatory and, in addition to exotic animals, such as bears and lions, also included dogs. This shows, once again, that not only the legal categories, but also biological ones, were quite variable, with no absolute.

Even in *Edictum de feris*, the subjective element is not referred to the animal, but to the human who performs the action (to carry) and that, therefore, assumes responsibility for its own; this remedy was not available in the case of free wild animals, since they were not subjected to any human control.

As in Roman law, wild animals are considered *res nullius*—no responsibility can be attributed to any human being for any damage or injury caused by them.

Actions for Damages for the Harm Caused to the Animals

The opposite of the discipline of damages caused by animals is that of damages suffered by them; as already mentioned, in Roman law there was no form of protection for nonhumans, but they were considered as important as any other economic good, with consequential right of the owner to compensation for any damage caused to them.

Lex Aquilia de damno stated the right of the owner to compensation for death or injury. This law considers animals the same as human slaves, since the parameter used for the determination of the amount recoverable is the same.[18]

In the original formulation of the *Lex Aquilia*, there is no reference to guilt as intended in the modern law, while it uses the principle of "traceability," which the contemporary law defines strict liability, or, at least, *culpa levissima.*[19]

Even in this case, the animal is not considered as a subject with its own interests, but the injury or killing is relevant exclusively in regards to financial damage to the owner.

It is true that slaves and animals are taken into account apart from the discipline for damages relating to the generality of the res, but it is also true that the specific in question derives exclusively from functional considerations, escaping any ideological considerations.

Res or Subjects?

Is it therefore possible to say that Roman law considered animals *res*, or it would be more correct to say the opposite? It is definitely correct what Vincenzo Ferrara states:

> The modern thinking to animal as a thing, cannot be traced back to the Roman concept of the animal as 'res' because, at that time, the distinction between res and personae did not constitute a rigid opposition. In essence, the legal classification of the 'servus' through the use of the categories as currently intended, of object and subject of law, does not allow you to grasp the significance of the distinction, typical of Roman jurisprudence, between personae and res. In fact, in the Roman systematic the same being, the man, can be considered at the same time person and res. The ancient distinction, therefore, unlike the modern contrast, is a distinction between partitions so to say 'open.'[20]

However, if, on one hand, the analysis of Roman's legal institutions for non-humans denote the use of different criteria from the modern ones, it is also undeniable that, reasoning from contraries, there is no recognition of subjectivity in the legal status of animals.

The picture that emerges is, probably, that of atypical *res*, that is, objects with a *quid pluris* than inanimate ones, so it seems reasonable to conclude that, indeed, a reconciliation to one or another legal category in Roman law was essentially devoid of the ideological value of which the modern age loaded it, at least in Western law.

Romans did not have problems in recognizing the existence of nonhuman behaviors, voluntary and independent, but in practice, this has not in any way led to the recognition of their rights, nor duties of others.

Realistically, the controversy about nonhumans' subjectivity is a contemporary phenomenon, as are the demands for animal rights in particular, and those of human rights in general.

If it is certainly understandable that the contemporary dichotomy between *res* and person was not reflected exactly in Roman law, it is also true that there is no doubt that nonhumans, like the slaves, were considered property, and therefore freely available by the owners.

In conclusion, the principle expressed by Francione is correct, namely that the fundamental distinction between human and nonhuman is in the status of property of the latter[21] and that only the variation of this circumstance may determine an equalization between species.

In support of the above, we can consider that slavery, which in ancient Rome characterized individuals of every type[22] and that, instead, has come to approach a criterion of race/ethnicity in the modern era. The obstacle to the equalization of individuals was not represented by the legal position in the list of res, but by the inclusion in the group of properties subject to ownership.

Animals in Medieval Law

Even different is the conception of the animal in medieval law, which could be defined literally schizophrenic. On the one hand, both culture and laws of the time were closely marked by the supremacy and uniqueness of man in creation, while, on the other hand, all animals were subjected to trials.

The first documented case of a trial against nonhuman creatures dates back to 864, when the Diet of Worms condemned a swarm of bees guilty of having killed a man to death by smoke.[23]

Horses, dogs, pigs, cows, roosters, even worms and termites have been tried, convicted or acquitted, executed or pardoned; obviously, their defense was always led by humans, with human laws having been applied to them.

Often pigs were on the docket in the medieval processes, as guilty of having devoured children, but another very common accusation was referred to sexual conjunction with humans, as they were considered instruments of the Devil.[24]

Recognizing the practice of such a process for nonhumans would seem to show that the medieval law considered them persons, as humans, but it should be noted that the processes (and convictions) at that time also concerned inanimate objects[25] and that, therefore, it would be erroneous to conclude that the medieval law has ever recognized the subjectivity of nonhumans.

The peculiarity of animals and the law in the Middle Ages is also apparent from the fact that the first, while actionable, did not enjoy any rights; in fact, there was not any equivalency between humans and nonhumans.[26]

Like in the Roman law, even in the Middle Ages there is not any conceptual choice, about considering nonhumans as *res* or as persons, while they are treated as property; moreover, the anthropocentric model of Christian inspiration, at the base of the culture, prevented any different evolution.[27]

2.2 NONHUMAN ANIMALS IN MODERN AND CONTEMPORARY LAW

The Origin of Welfarism

With the evolution of industrial civilization, the world of human animals was separated almost completely from that of the nonhumans, whose interaction with man became based entirely on the premise of being taken away from their natural habitat, to be introduced in the artificial cities.

With the modern age, urban life spreads and the urban dimension assumes greater detachment from the natural environment. The relationship between "human citizens" and nonhumans occurs almost exclusively with domesticated animals, especially pets, and it is to them that the first legal address of Western history that attests the legislature's intent to protect them develops, regardless of economic interest due to them.

The symbol of the American Society for the Prevention of Cruelty to Animals (ASPCA), founded in 1866, is a horse lying on the ground, attacked by the driver of a wagon with a stick[28] , which shows that the first instances of animal protection are born by social disapproval of those phenomena evident and socially distributed, at a time when the conduct of animal-drawn transport was the only form of transport possible and was widely practiced.

In the cities, "coachmen" were the equivalent of modern taxis and these, in order to maximize profits from transporting paying passengers, tended to abuse the horses that pulled the wagons, often spurring them and beating them with such a violence that passers were scared.

The first legal transposition of the feelings of those people who disapproved the public beatings of animals occurs in 1641, when the Massachusetts General Court states: *"No man shall exercise any tyranny or cruelty towards any brute creatures which are usually kept for man's use*[29] *."*

The institute is generic and does not contain any indication of what is meant by either *tyranny* or *cruelty*, nor what animals are protected; about the last question, though, the criterion chosen is that of animals *"kept for man's use."* It is neither pet nor domesticated animals, while the term *"use"* could regard even those used for food purposes, in which case, though, the mistreatment condemned would obviously be the so-called *"useless cruelty."*

The case of the Court of Massachusetts was destined to remain isolated for almost two centuries, since the first actual coding of a similar rule dates back to 1822, when England's Cruel Treatment of Cattle Act takes into account human behaviors against certain nonhumans, condemning the acts of cruelty.

The rule defines an exhaustive list of protected animals (horses, mules, donkeys, bulls, cows, steers, and sheep), which expressly prohibits them from being *"cruelly beat, abused, or ill-treated*[30] *."* This inaugurates the age of the laws for animal welfare, a symptom of the legislative policy that Francione has not hesitated to define as schizophrenia.[31]

As with the Court's ruling in Massachusetts, the use or killing of animals for economic purposes do not find any restriction; actually, it is limited to just the exercising of acts deliberately cruel that are unrelated to the owner's purposes.

The abovementioned law implies the duties "indirect," namely those duties that are not already set up to "directly" protect nonhumans, while the interest protected is the human sense of mercy.

The evolution of the institute, in 1835, led to the adoption of the Cruelty To Animals Act[32], laying down a complex discipline to regulate not only the conduct toward cattle, but also a multitude of other species.

The main innovation of this law, which makes it a true milestone in Western law, is an express provision of mandatory fulfillments for the protection of animals, while up to that time only the mistreatment (as an active conduct) was sanctioned.

The owner or keeper of animals becomes punishable for having, for example, failed to feed them properly, causing illness or death.

The Legal Status of Animals in Italian Law

After noting that Italian law qualifies all nonhumans as *res*, not knowing the intermediate category between things and people, we should note that there is a subdivision within this category, connected with the concept of ownership.

Pursuant to art. 810 of the Civil Code *"are goods the things that can be objects of rights."* Among these, by definition, are included without distinction all nonhuman animals, regardless of species.

In accordance with governing laws and regulations, all nonhumans, like objects in general (as equivalent to them) may be owned by someone or all (*res nullius*), in which case they may be taken freely by anyone; at least until 1977 Italian law fully implemented this principle.

The situation has changed, and the legislature has established a demarcation between objects in general and animals in particular, with the enactment of the law 968/77 about wildlife; this law applies to all those animals that are not traditionally considered domestic or pet.

Article 1 of law 968/77 states that wildlife *"is unavailable heritage of the state and is protected as interest of the national community."*[33] Here arises the new classification of animals in Italian law, which, while keeping intact the status of things, recognizes two possible conditions, alternatives to each other—private property or public property.

If, in conceptual terms, considering animals as things of one kind or another does not result in significant consequences, in practice, the fact that wild animals are counted among the goods unavailable of the nation has many consequences. First, unlike *res nullius*, they are not freely disposable, since any act of disposal must be determined (or, at least, allowed) by local authorities, while, in the absence of such authorization, one who takes possession of a wild animal commits the crime of theft. [34]

The rationale underlying the law 968/77 is the subtraction of wildlife from free and indiscriminate availability by individuals; recognizing the legal status of public good, the right/duty to provide is attributed to the government.

As custodians, the state, and, in particular, local authorities are obliged to protect the *res communes omnium*. If, on the one hand, they can dispose of them, on the other hand, they are responsible for ensuring the integrity[35] and bear the responsibility.[36]

Not only wild animals, but all nonhumans that are not privately owned are considered public domain, including even those traditionally defined as "domestic" or "pet," such as stray dogs and cats.

As, in fact, completely unrelated to collective sentiment, even the appropriation of an animal as "domestic" roaming (stray) in the territory of any city, representing an act of disposal of a public asset, should be authorized in advance by local authorities.[37]

Rules Governing the Treatment of Animals in Italy

The nineteenth century in Europe, with its intellectual ferment and relevant socio-political and economic changes, marks, on one hand, the dissemination of the principles of animal protection, and, on the other hand, the affirmation of the principle of indirect duties; it is not a coincidence that the birth of the so-called "zoophilia" is placed in this period, namely, the interest in animals that does not match (necessarily) attention for their real welfare, as the observation, study, etc.

Italy was not an exception, and in 1856 the Grand Duchy of Tuscany issued a first rule, a penal law, devoted to animals and followed by that, similar, of the Grand Duchy of Sardinia in 1859: both prohibit cruelty toward pets in public places.[38]

Article. 685 n. 7 of the Sardinian Code of 1859-91 stated: *"Fall in contravention those who, in public places, make cruel acts against pets."*[39] .

To constitute a crime, in short, it was necessary that the abuse was perpetrated against pets and that it affected public sentiment of compassion, while the aggression of animals at home could not have been sanctioned.

The penal code Zanardelli, the first adopted by Italy, united and entered into force in 1890, receives almost slavishly the Savoy legislation, introducing the art. 491's provision, according to which: *"Whoever becomes cruel to animals or, without need, mistreats or forces them to manifestly excessive labors, shall be punished by a fine of up to one hundred pounds.*

"The same penalty is the one who, even if only for scientific or educational purpose, but out of places for teaching, bring animals to experiments such as to create disgust."

The basic distinctions between Zanardelli and Sardinian Code are the expunction of the phrases: *"in public places"* and *"pets."* These changes had been strongly desired by the Minister of Justice in relation to the Code: *"The cruelty to animals (that there is no reason to limit, how does the Sardinian Code, to domestic species) must be condemned and forbidden because the tormenting spirit with ruthless sentient beings, bringing them proud torment, does not cease to be bad because those who suffer from it are devoid of human reason."*[40]

A few years after the first Italian penal code, in 1913, Law no. 611, entitled Provisions for the Protection of Animals[41] was enacted. The first article illustrates and adds an additional adaption to those already in place, pursuant to art. 491, reaching to prohibit *"unnecessary torture for the industrial exploitation of each animal species."*

In particular art. 2 c) with regard to the allocation of legal associations, talks about *"educating the population not using harshness towards animals"* and *"giving the school special instructions on the need to protect animals."* The scope of such conceptual expressions is much broader than that underlying the expression *"feeling of love for animals,"* and it seems to take into account animals for their intrinsic value, rather than for human appreciation.

The 1913 law, however, has found little application, both for the historical context unlucky (the First World War), and the apparent lack of an appropriate cultural background where the seeds of a culture animal could sprout.

Article 491 of Zanardelli will then be transfused art. 727 of the Code of Rocco (1930), among the offenses: its reform will come with the law no. 189/04, which introduced into the Criminal Code the Title IX *bis*, dedicated to *"offenses against the feeling for animals,"* and Articles 544 *bis-sexies* of the Penal Code.[42]

Through the enactment of Law 189/04, strongly supported by some associations for animal rights, animal abuse, which was a breach, became an offense and penalties have been increased.

Article 544 *ter*, currently in force, contains the precepts laid down in previous Article 727 (now referred exclusively to the abandonment of animals) and provides: *"Whoever, for cruelty or unnecessarily causes an injury to an animal or submit it to torture or conduct or toil or work unbearable for its ethological characteristics shall be punished with imprisonment from three months to one year or a fine of 3.000 to 15.000 euros."*

More severe sanctions are imposed by article 544 *bis* for the killing of animals: *"Whoever, for cruelty or unnecessarily, causes the death of an animal, shall be punished with imprisonment from three months to eighteen months.*"

The concepts of *cruelty* and *unnecessary*, already characteristic of nineteenth-century codes, remain the criterion of *ethological characteristics* as a benchmark of the illegal conduct introduced for the first time.

There is no reference to the sentient nature of animals, and the placement does not give rise to misunderstandings; the principle of indirect duties is confirmed by the title of the book, which defines the human feeling that protected interest.

The Italian legislation reflects Francione's concept of legislative schizophrenia, since it is adherent to the model of law that enshrines protection on the one hand and, on the other hand, subordinates this protection to economic considerations that, in fact, prevail. [43]

What Francione argued, in particular with reference to the practice of the use of nonhumans for food, which he considers a fundamental starting point for the recognition of any animal rights, is readily observed in the Italian legislation—a rigorous definition, in fact, might conclude that even the slaughter for food is forbidden, as not dictated by need and consistent in the death of animals.

To prevent extensive interpretations of the law, the Italian legislator has introduced the exceptions in article no. 3 of the law 189/04, providing the introduction of art. 19b in the coordination and transitional provisions of the Penal Code:

> Special laws relating to animals.—The provisions of Title IX-bis of Book II of the Penal Code shall not apply to the cases provided for by special laws on hunting, fishing, breeding, transport, slaughter of animals, scientific experimentation on them, of activities circus, zoological gardens, as well as other special laws relating to animals. The provisions of Title IX-bis of Book II of the Penal Code do not apply equally to the historical and cultural events authorized by the competent region. [44]

Notwithstanding that even the L 189/04 has not given any legal subjectivity to nonhumans, it could be stated that, in the absence of such a derogation, the definition could be applied to slaughter.

If, in fact, it is true that the vision or the simple awareness of injured animals, killed or otherwise suffering, causes suffering to humans, it is also undeniable that the slaughter involves both the suffering and the killing and that, therefore, it harms the protected interest repeatedly.

The exceptions not only in food, but also with reference to hunting and historical events, shows that even in this case the legislature intended to protect human habits and the economic use of nonhumans.

In Italian criminal law, there is a norm, article 638 Penal Code, which, by applying the principles of the ancient institution *Lex Aquilia de damno*, covers offenses as killing animals of others. This rule is part of the heritage protection, taking up the traditional meaning *animal = asset.*

The relationships among different Italian criminal laws on the subject of abuse/killing of animals are clarified in the case law of the Supreme Court:

> The context of article 638 Penal Code in the reworked text of the law n. 189 of 2004, stands out from the crime under article 544-ter Penal Code and the contravention of article 727 Penal Code, as, although they coincide by the objective element (when it is in the presence of pets), changes the subjective element consisting in the offense under article 638 Penal Code, conscience and desire to produce, without the need, deterioration, damage or killing of animals of others. Different is also the legal right protected by the three incriminating rules, because, unlike the contravention of article 727 Penal Code *ante novellam* and the crime under article 544-ter, in which is protected the feeling for animals, the case of article 638 Penal Code protects the animal as asset and therefore requires, as a constituent element of the crime, the consciousness of the animal's property by a third party, who is victim of the crime(Court of Cassation pen. Sect. III Sent., 24/10/2007, no. 44822)

The judgment of the Supreme Court does not seem to give rise to any dispute of interpretation and establishes effectively both the rationale and the scope of applicability of the laws examined.

Compared to Roman law, the Italian waiver of any conceptual neutrality states unequivocally that the award of a form of protection for nonhumans does not give them any legal subjectivity, representing only a duty of respect for humans of a feeling, also human.

It might be asked why the contemporary law felt the need of schematization and classification that was lacking in the Roman world. As pointed out by Bobbio, the contemporary age has experienced and is experiencing the affirmation of the concept of human rights as has never before occurred.[45]

Italian law seems to adhere perfectly to Bobbio's theoretical enunciation and, with regard to relations with nonhumans, it also seems to reflect Pisanò's thought, which gleans in the humanistic anthropocentrism the foundation of the so-called *dehumanized rights.*[46]

Comparing the hypothesis of Pisanò with contemporary law, noted that currently there has been no recognition of real rights in favor of any nonhuman subject, it might be concluded that this is at an intermediate stage between the manifestation of values and their elevation to the rank of genuine individual rights.[47]

The recourse to the expedient of "*human feeling*" by the Italian legislature allows us to recognize at the same time certain instances of animals' protection, and established habits (especially economic activities).

The Italian legislative system fully implements welfarism, failing to recognize any right to nonhumans. Such recognition, as we have seen, would be incompatible with their status of things and, therefore, in the future, could be envisaged two alternative ways—or elevate animals to the status of legal entities, while maintaining the internal consistency of the regulatory framework and, therefore, renouncing to any form of use inconsistent with this condition, or give up the conceptual coherence and establish a bipartite system able to reconcile the establishment of "some" rights with the perpetuation of a model, however, based on anthropocentrism. [48]

Instrumental Law

The concept of animals as *res*, that within the legal framework described above is more and more strong today, is reaffirmed in Italian law through a series of technical laws regulating certain human activities involving animals; it is the case of Presidential Decree no. 320/54 (Veterinary Police Regulations) that establishes the methods to isolate and deal with cases of contagious diseases in animals in the herd. [49]

In recent decades, the spread of bovine spongiform or so-called *bird flu* have resulted in the frequent use of the abovementioned health practices: the more frequent intervention was killing, which affected millions of animals [50] ; as the Ministry of Health indicates, the killing *"will be preferentially selective but can also be total if authorized by the Directorate General of Animal Health and Veterinary Medicine, Ministry of Health."* [51]

Both the ministerial legislation and interpretation show the status of res of so-called *production animals*, regulating (even) the killing without any acknowledgment of subjectivity.

The comparison between legal institutions of "protection" and those of veterinary policy shows that Italian law, in relating to nonhumans, has not adopted a philosophical or biological policy, but rather, eminently practical. The distinction between animals to "protect" and the others focuses essentially on their intended use.

The conceptual distinction among nonhuman categories is particularly evident in the law no. 281/91, the Framework Law of companion animals and prevention of stray dogs. [52]

Article 1 of law 281/91 shows the intentions of the Legislature: *"The State shall promote and regulate the protection of pet animals, condemns the acts of cruelty against them, ill-treatment and their abandonment, in order to promote the proper coexistence between man and to protect animal and public health and the environment."*

Law 281/91 anticipated in many respects the law 189/04 and, more importantly, has intervened to change the discipline of stray animals (pets not held by humans), marking an end to the indiscriminate removal or use for vivisection and transforming the kennels in shelters, resulting in the abandonment of the previous system, which provided the killing of animals not adopted.[53]

The European Union Framework

So far, the Community legislation about nonhumans is expressed mainly in two directions: on the one hand, the regulation of certain specific cases, and, on the other hand, the externalization of broad principles without binding and completely abstracted from positive law.

Certainly, these are referable to the first kind the European Convention for the Protection of Animals kept for Farming Purposes (1976) and the Convention for the Protection of Animals for Slaughter (1979), transposed in Italy by law no. 623/85.[54]

About slaughter, the *ratio legis* is well expressed in article 2, paragraph 4 of the Strasbourg Convention of May 10, 1979: *"Save the animals slaughtered in a slaughterhouse or out of them any avoidable pain or suffering."*[55] The aims are pursued through the provision of appropriate methods, compliance with which is required by all Member States, to ensure the least possible suffering to animals before slaughter.

The term *"unnecessary suffering"* (or equivalent) is often used in the European legislation as a dividing line between what is allowed and what is not; the utility parameter is clearly referring to the advantage that human beings (or at least some of them) can receive from the suffering caused to animals, insomuch that it is not prohibited in absolute terms, but only on the condition that it is unnecessary, namely not productive of beneficial effects for the agent (human) that causes it.

On abstract and ideological levels, the European regulations introduced by the Treaty of Lisbon, which approved the modification of the Treaty on European Union, article 13 now states that:

> In formulating and implementing the Union's agriculture, fisheries, transport, internal market, research and technological development and space policies, the Union and the Member States shall full account of the welfare of animals as sentient beings, while respecting the legislative or administrative provisions and customs of Member States relating in particular to religious rites, cultural traditions, and regional heritage.[56]

Animals, therefore, are recognized as "sentient beings" and not as mere objects. This would seem to lead to more extensive protection, but the following period clarifies the limits of that consideration, reiterating its subordination to any human interest and, in particular, those arising from religion and culture.

What has been and what will be, therefore, the practical implications of this statement of principle on the legal subjectivity of animals, which emerges as unique in the regulatory west landscape?

In the first place, the *action plan for the welfare of animals* received impetus and new conceptual tools: this plan, originally scheduled for four years, 2006-2010, has taken certain objectives in relation to different types of relationships between man and animals, intending in each case to improve the welfare of nonhumans involved.

Purpose and Method of the four-year plan are accurately described by Stefano Grassi, who pointed out that in this regard:

> The main objective of the program of action was to ensure that the activities in the field of animal welfare, take account their cross-sectoral nature, their size, and their European and international values, and the range of skills associated and inter-which are necessarily involved [...] identifying the need for a coordinated and holistic approach to this issue also, by the method of gradualism and balancing, which are evidence of the actions identified. [57]

If, on the one hand, the determinations of the Lisbon Treaty are placed far beyond the provisions of the national law of animals, and, in particular, establish the legal subjectivity that many have claimed as an inevitable starting point for the recognition of real rights for nonhumans, on the other hand, the European framework, starting from the abovementioned four-year plan, has not abandoned the principle of welfarism.

The choice of the term "welfare" in the plan of the European Union implies the rejection of the abolitionist model, in favor, rather, of a regulation of the use of nonhumans, intended to limit the suffering.

Under Italian law, a first relapse, conceivably due to the Treaty of Lisbon, is apparent in the order of 16.7.09 of the Ministry of Labour, Health, and Social Policy, which sought to intervene in the matter of *"entrusting the service of custody and management, by the municipalities, of stray dogs under their responsibility in accordance with regulations."* [58]

As pointed out by Pisanò

> it is a rule which, although secondary, also poses the problem of sorting in our consideration of the subjectivity of the animals. In contrast, in fact, the provisions of the L 189/2004 for the protection of animals leaving, however, from the human perspective, the ordinance in question is centered around the individual and specific 'welfare of animals as sentient beings.' [59]

2.3 THE RELATIONSHIP BETWEEN HUMANS AND
NONHUMANS IN COMPARATIVE LAW

Italian legislative experience in the field of animals is not isolated, but is part of a context, the European and Western, which, during the last two centuries, has evolved in a similar way and that, despite the differences in legislations—sometimes significant—reflects the relationship of Western man with animals.

Examining the foreign legal institutions provides more comprehension on the historical evolution of the human-animal relationship, thus allowing us to imagine what could be the future paths and reflections on what they will have to begin.

Although the approach to the matter is uniformed, there are certain peculiarities far from negligible, demonstrating different cultural traditions, religious and moral.

If the laws applied in European countries seem to have a common theoretical matrix, which determines a similar approach to the "animal question," the comparison with the US legal institutions shows more differences, probably due to three factors: first, a different legal tradition, even compared to the English from which they derive, as well as a separate cultural matrix, and, finally, different relationships between economics and politics.

French Law

Article 521-1 of the French Penal Code reads that: *"fait publiquement ou non, of exercer des sevices graves, ou sexuelle de nature, ou de commettre an acte de Cruauté envers un animal domestique, apprivoisé ou, ou tenu en captivité, est puni de deux ans d'emprisonnement et de 30000 euros d'amende*[60] (the fact of engaging in, publicly or not, serious physical or sexual abuse, or commit an act of cruelty to a pet or domesticated, or held in captivity, is punishable by two years' imprisonment and a fine of 30.000 euros)."

Even in comparison with the Zanardelli, it emerges in the gap of the French Code, which fails to protect wild animals in any way, but merely considers only those who, for whatever reason, are held by man. It seems to be a precise legislative policy choice, which is intended to leave to humans the full and free availability of wildlife.

Among fines, article R654-1 includes the conduct of mistreatment of animals, which is distinguished from the abovementioned crime. It speaks of *"sans nécessité, publiquement ou non, of exercer volontairement traitements des mauvais* (without any necessity, exercise voluntarily abuse, publicly or not)." It excluded the applicability of the rule in question in cases of bullfights and cockfights, where these are manifestations of "*uninterrupted local tradition.*"

Unlike what is found in the Italian Penal Code, contextualization within the French Code does not provide any parameter useful for interpretation, since institutions are qualified as separate cases and not included in other, larger, protections or under headings or titles.

As in the Italian legislation, there is no prediction—explicit or implicit—about the use of animals for food; it might, therefore, be wondered whether the killing for this purpose can configure that *serious abuse*, as such suitable to consider this as the existence of the prohibited conduct.

If it is true that the rule in question has considerable resemblance to that equivalent of Italian law, it is also true that, unlike the latter, the French legislature did not provide any of the exceptions—such as killing for food—used in Italy to limit the scope of the law.

In France, the issue of animal protection institute has not given any ban or limit to the use of nonhumans for fun, food, etc. It seems, therefore, that we must conclude that, even in the presence of a law that, strictly speaking, would be perfectly applicable to any relationship between humans and nonhumans, the limitation is implied, and derogations even taken for granted by the legislature.

Spanish Law

The article 337 of the Codigo Penal represents the fundamental discipline in the field of animal protection in Spain:

> Los que maltrataren with ensañamiento and injustificadamente to animales domésticos causándoles provocándoles lesiones que la muerte or produzcan a serious menoscabo físico Serán castigados with the penalty Prisión de tres meses de año and a inhabilitación especial de tres años para one el ejercicio de profesión, oficio or Commercial que takes relación con los animales[61] (those who mistreat cruelly and unjustly pets, causing death or causing such injuries that cause to them a severe physical disability, shall be punished with imprisonment from three months to a year and special disqualification from one to three years from the exercise of the profession, office, or business connected with animals, Ed.).

The Spanish law for the protection of animals is part of Chapter IV, under the heading dedicated to the "*protection of flora, fauna, and pets,*" contained in the title XVI, "*crimes related to the order of the territory and the protection of the historical and environmental heritage.*" The choice of the legislature, unlike the Italian, was therefore to transpose the mistreatment of animals not so much as an infringement of human feelings, but rather of the natural heritage of which they are considered part.

Not even in this case could it be considered any establishment of genuine individual rights of nonhuman animals, though the different legal categorization implies a different approach, more open to the recognition of an intrinsic value that disregards the appreciation of humans.

English Law

English law, strengthened also by the increased political stability in recent centuries, has continually updated the rules on the protection of animals, dating back to the dawn of the nineteenth century, updating them and adapting to the times. The law Protection of Animals Act was enacted in 1911, and it was significantly changed in 1968 and again in 1986.[62]

English law, among European ones, is definitely more analytical, listing some of the conduct penalized and expressly distinguishing between commissive and omissive, as well as providing to the police specific powers of intervention, also surrogate, to rescue or euthanize animals whose owners are unaccounted for, against or inert.

Section 1 defines the mistreatment:

> "Cruelly beat, kick, ill-treat, over-ride, over-drive, over-load, torture, infuriate, or terrify any animal, or shall cause or procure, or, being the owner, permit any animal to be so used, or shall, by wantonly or unreasonably doing or omitting to do any act, or causing or procuring the commission or omission of any act, cause any unnecessary suffering, or, being the owner, permit any unnecessary suffering to be so caused to any animal."[63]

In this case, as in the French Code or German one, there is no conceptual reference, and the matter is regulated independently. It would not seem fair to say that the system has accepted the so-called indirect duties, since in some cases it is even stated that authorities can "override" the feeling of the owner of the animal, where it is considered to be contrary to the interest of the latter.[64]

The main limitation of the discipline is probably the large arbitrariness underlying the concept of "unnecessary suffering," the definition of which is left entirely to the judge on the basis of each individual case. The anthropocentric perspective is clear, however, since it is *in re ipsa* that the principle of necessity regards eminently human interests and also requires a subjective interpretation.

Unlike Spanish law, it is impossible to consider the Protection of Animals Act based on the ideal that animals belong to nature, since section 15 of the standard (Definitions), expressly declares that: *"The expression 'animal' means any domestic or captive animal,"* thus excluding any wildlife preservation.

The definition could still include the animals used for food as, certainly, those are in the condition of captivity. In this regard, point three of the same section one states that the provisions of the Act do not apply *"to the commission or omission of any act in the course of the destruction, or the preparation for destruction, of any animal as food for mankind, Unless longer available destruction or longer available preparation was accompanied by the infliction of unnecessary suffering."*

Even in this case, as in the Italian law no. 189/04, is the same rule to provide exceptions and, in particular, one that allows the systematized activities of suppression for food.

The forms of wildlife are protected under English law through the Wildlife and Countryside Act 1981, that, in Section 9, states: *"If any person intentionally or recklessly kills, injures, or takes any wild animal included in Schedule 5, shall he be guilty of an offense."*

The difference between protection of wild and domestic animals seems to be rooted in the socio-historical origins of the first, the original formulation which dates back to 1822 and was intended to prevent those abuses that were usual in the urban context.

The scope of English law, as well as the number and extent of provisions and the absence of conceptual foreclosures, such as a limit to human feeling, rather than ecological usefulness of nonhuman, make it more open to the recognition of real animal rights, so that it has been provided a special exception to allow the slaughter.

German Law

German legislation provided a real regulatory apparatus dedicated to nonhuman animals and called Tiereschutzgesetz.[65] In this *corpus*, consisting of twenty-two articles, all the fundamental aspects of relationships between species are regulated in a unified way, including the system of sanctions in the case of violations.

Article 1 defines issues such as well-being and ill-treatment as Italian law no. 189/04, recognizing animals as living creatures and, as such, liable to experience well-being.

The main difference between German and Italian law is the articulation of the first, which refers explicitly to the obligations in human-nonhuman relationships, looking specifically at the compulsory treatment in the case of breeding (articles 2-3 and 11-12), abatement (articles 4-4b), surgical operations (articles 5-6a), the trial (articles 7-9a), as well as aspects such as the reproduction and measures for the protection of animals, whereas articles 17 provide the penalty system, which includes both imprisonment and fine in the case of murder or ill-treatment.

On the sidelines of Tiereschutzgesetz's penal provisions, article 90 of BGB states: "*Animals are not things*," though the second paragraph of the rule specifies that "*unless otherwise specified, the requirements applicable to the things are equally valid for the animals.*"

German laws regarding nonhuman animals represent a sort of bridge between the legal positions of continental Europe and English ones; in fact, similar to the latter, German law provides a comprehensive discipline, taking into account specific reports.

On the other hand, it is clear that the German legislature was confronted with the legal approach, typical of continental Europe, which maintains the traditional dichotomy: *res*/subject.

The BGB, denying the animal status of simple things, but failing to recognize real rights, could represent a sort of third way, an alternative to persons and things; perhaps that is what Varner described as the category of almost persons? Indeed, in this case, it would be more fitting to Varner's third category, namely that of merely sentient beings, but we should underline that German law omits any inclusive definition, merely stating what animals "are not," but does not go so far as to determine "what" (or "whom") they are.

US Law

The first legal protection of animals was born in the United States nearly four centuries ago. It would be presumed, therefore, that laws of that country are the most advanced, or, at least, that they can offer interesting insights as to the recognition of real animal rights.

The USA is a federation of states, and each of them has significant legislative powers in many areas. The protection of animals is no exception and, in fact, the only federal law (and therefore common to all states) that regulates the treatment of animals in research, shows, transport, and trade, is the Animal Welfare Act[66], enacted in 1966 and subsequently amended and supplemented several times (last in 2010), together with the Animal Welfare Regulations.[67]

The title, with reference to welfare, refers to the noted contrast between rights and simple concessions, leading to the conclusion that it supports the latter category.

The normative text is extremely complex and is intended to provide minimum standards of treatment related to specific human activities conducted on/with animals, while there is no correlation with the repression of ill-treatment, that is at the center of European laws mentioned above.

As in Europe, no reference to vegetarianism, direct or indirect, can be found in US federal law, while the Humane Methods of Slaughter Act[68] is designed to regulate the slaughter with its "humane" methods, based on the principle expressed in section 1901:

The Congress that finds the use of humane methods in the slaughter of live-stock prevents needless suffering, results in safer and better working conditions for persons engaged in the slaughtering industry, brings about improvement of products and economies in slaughtering operations, produces and other benefits for producers, processors, and which consumers tend to expedite an orderly flow of livestock and livestock products in interstate and foreign commerce.

Also in the American law system, the rules on the protection of animals are contained in the Criminal Code and, as each state has the legislative power, each of them adopted a different and independent discipline, sometimes extremely varied.

Californian culture is an example at the forefront of animal rights, so it is interesting to analyze its laws. Here is a very articulated protection, contained in paragraphs 596, 597, and following of the Penal Code.[69]

The § 597 sets forth the prohibitions: "*Every person who maliciously and intentionally maims, mutilates, tortures, or wounds a living animal, or maliciously and intentionally kills an animal, is guilty of an offense.*"

The following § 599b clarifies the protected subjects and the interpretation of the terms used: "*every dumb creature, the words 'torment,' 'torture,' and 'cruelty' include every act, omission, or neglect whereby unnecessary or unjustifiable physical pain or suffering is caused or permitted.*"

Particularly original is the definition of protected subjects, as "*all creatures devoid of speech,*" which is a *unicum* with respect to the European regulatory landscape, and is able to encompass all forms of animal life, far from being limited to domestic animals/wildlife.

The reference to moral sufferings, as well as physical ones, seems to militate in favor of a legislature's choice more prone to direct duties instead of indirect, recognizing the subjectivity of nonhuman animals.

It is also missing any reference to the criterion of necessity, and such omission seems to underlie a choice of the legislature prone to theoretical equivalence between the interests of human and nonhuman animals.

Once the animal's right to an independent life is stated and, in the absence of higher-level antagonistic interests and the exemption represented by the criterion of "necessity," it could be argued about the issue of vegetarianism as an obligation, but even in this case, there is an express derogation about killing for food (§ 599):

No part of this title shall be construed as interfering with any of the laws of this state known as the 'game laws,' or any laws for or against the destruction of certain birds, nor must this title be construed as interfering with the right to destroy any venomous reptile, or any animal known as dangerous to life, limb, or property, or to interfere with the right to kill all animals used for food, or with properly conducted scientific experiments or investigations performed

under the authority of the faculty of a regularly incorporated medical college
or university of this state.

In conclusion, the legal status of nonhuman animals in the United States,
though largely left to the laws of individual states, in general, presents considerable formal differences with respect to the formulation of European
rules governing the same field, but these differences, in practical terms, are
less important than the similarities; many Western legal systems recognize a
treatment of nonhuman animals that, admitting fledged economic exploitation, just tends to banish those ill-treatment "unnecessary."[70]

2.4 ANIMAL RIGHTS AND CONSTITUTION AROUND THE WORLD

To Constitutionalize or Not to Constitutionalize?

The objective of constitutionalizing animal rights and, therefore, recognizing
them as inalienable and fundamental rights, has been pursued by some animal advocates around the world for a long time—some of these efforts suc-
ceeded, particularly in Germany and in Switzerland.

There is also an open debate about the same opportunity to make animal
rights recognized by the Constitution; that would imply elevating them to the
same level as human rights. Many people are scared by that possibility—how
could we manage or balance our interests when they are opposed to those of
animals?

Some constitutional experts have expressed skepticism about the possibility of including animal rights in the Constitution:

> The compression of human rights by the Constitution may happen only if it is
> necessary to the realization of other human rights or public interests, related to
> the first. With a joke, believe that constitutionalism is incompatible with the
> rodent as a measure violated the right to life of the mice, it would be a
> laughable assertion that no lawyer would even dare to move forward. It must
> therefore be concluded that the constitutionalism leads to the configuration of
> animal rights, but not in terms that could lead to constitutional status of equal-
> ity between humans and other species.[71]

Here, we are going to examine if and how it is possible to recognize
animal rights at a constitutional level, and how we should handle conflicts
between human and animal rights.

The Western World, even full of differences, is actually very alike when
it comes to animal rights issues, and the experiences of those countries that
have recognized them in their Constitutions may be very useful to make a
forecast.

We will see what happened in Germany and Switzerland, and how they included animals in their Constitutions, as well as the Italian and US proposals, which represent two different approaches to the same issue. While the first is aimed to amend an existing law, the second is intended to found a brand new Constitution, entirely dedicated to animals, and that, in many aspects, reflects the "human" Bill of Rights.

If it is true that animals cannot formally enter into any contract, it is true that they are not to make any claims against the man, but rather the contrary: when human beings claim, for example, the right to eat animals or hunt them for entertainment, there is no equivalency.

The fundamental assumption of any Constitution is in recognition of the principles of equality, reciprocity, equal dignity; these documents have sometimes perpetuated discrimination, but they never established new or expanded existing ones.

The right to vote, for example, was gradually extended, but always through formulations of positive type, designed to broaden the application of the institution (by wealth, gender, etc.) and never, in contrast, by narrowing it.

In conclusion, the juxtaposition animal rights/human rights does not seem correct in the constitutional framework, since any legal construction is necessarily an abstraction by the legislator, which will necessarily be founded and limited in itself and for itself. As Bobbio also pointed out, the allocation of rights different from those uniquely human, may also find a place in a system of values eminently anthropocentric, as an expression of a widespread desire.[72]

The European Union Frame

For the first time in the European Community history, in 1992, a declaration on animal welfare was annexed to the revised Treaty of Maastricht.

The 1999 Amsterdam Treaty included a protocol on animal welfare. That protocol required[73] EU policy makers to pay "full regard" to animal welfare when adopting legislation in a number of policy areas.

In 2009 the text of the protocol was incorporated in the text of the Lisbon Treaty, as Article 13. This puts animal welfare on the same footing as other key principles, such as promoting gender equality, guaranteeing social protection, protecting human health, combating discrimination, promoting sustainable development, ensuring consumer protection, and protecting personal data.

The Lisbon Treaty states that:

> In formulating and implementing the Union's agriculture, fisheries, transport, internal market, research and technological development and space policies,

> the Union and the Member States shall, since animals are sentient beings, pay full regard to the welfare requirements of animals, while respecting the legislative or administrative provisions and customs of the Member States relating in particular to religious rites, cultural traditions, and regional heritage.

While the above represents one of the only official recognitions of animals as sentient beings in the Western World, it also maintains animal exploitation as an unquestionable issue, and, therefore, is very similar to welfare laws. In other words, while the EU statement may appear as a legal recognition of animals as actual right-holders, this is not, and their condition as property is confirmed.

The European animal welfare laws that are not directly affected by the abovesaid statement may already be considered consistent with it, since even if they do not formally recognize the sentient nature of nonhumans, they do already limit their mistreatment.

The 2002 German Constitutional Reform

On July 26th, 2002, in Germany, the reform of the *Grundgesetz* was approved, which led to a new wording of article 20a, aimed at introducing the protection of animals among the basics:

> Der Staat schützt auch in Verantwortung für die künftigen Generationen die natürlichen Lebensgrundlagen und die Tiere im Rahmen der verfassungsmäßigen Ordnung durch die Gesetzgebung und nach Maßgabe von Gesetz und Recht durch die vollziehende Gewalt und die Rechtsprechung (The state shall protect, as a responsibility toward future generations, the natural foundations of life and animals as part of the constitutional order, through legislation and in accordance with law and justice by the executive and the judiciary, Ed.)

The legislative intervention consisted in the addition of the words "*und die Tiere*" (*and animals*, Ed.) to the ranks of the protections offered in the name of future generations; the wording has been taken in some of the Italian constitutional bills seen above. [74]

Article 20a, stating an obligation of the State to "protect," does not introduce any absolute parameter and impassive interpretation, but, on the contrary, leaves the definition of "protection" to the interpreter.

The German reform has its roots in the first half of the '90s of the last century. In 1994 and subsequently in 1997 and 2000, in fact, there were many attempts to introduce the change, but the opposition parties of the Centre had frustrated such attempts. The change on 2002 was possibly thanks to the Constitutional Court decision that recognized the right to perform ritual slaughter to the Islamic community, notwithstanding the current law.

In practice, the interpretation of the concept of "protection" of nonhumans in Germany seems quite comparable to that of the former Italian definition, by the law no. 189/04, remitted to the social feeling. In fact, the activities related to the use of nonhumans by humans are not ceased, but, if anything, have been regulated and sometimes limited in a similar way to what happens in other Western countries.

It is clear that the German reform, although literally equalizing human and animal rights on the paper, did not change anything in concrete terms, as animals are still subject to human decisions and will.

Even after the abovesaid amendment, animals in Germany are still hunted, sold, bought, killed, eaten, etc.; despite the Constitutional rank of their "rights," the animals in Germany are still protected under mere laws, as happens in other Western countries.

This experience makes two things clear:

1. the mere recognition of animal rights by the Constitution does not imply actual differences in their treatment, nor in their conditions;
2. the same possibility of conflict between human rights and animal rights is prevented by the fact that only the social feeling can determine the effectiveness of a law (even at the constitutional level), and it is unthinkable that the human society dismiss its rights in favor of those of animals.

The 1973 Swiss Constitu*tional Reform*

If the *Grundgesetz* adopted a general formulation about animal rights, conversely the Federal Constitution of the Swiss Confederation has opted for a specific discipline (dating 1973), contained in sections 79 and 80, respectively titled "Fishing and hunting" and "Protection of animals." Article 79 states:

> The Confederation shall establish principles on the exercise of fishing and hunting, in particular to preserve the diversity of species of fish, wild mammals, and birds." Article 80 states: "The Confederation shall legislate on the protection of animals. 2 Discipline, in particular: a. the keeping and care of animals, b. experiments and intervention on live animals c. the use of animals; d. the importation of animals and animal products, and trade and transport of animals; f. the killing of animals. 3 The cantons are responsible for implementation of the requirements, as the law does not reserve to the Confederation.

Compared to the German constitutional provision, the Swiss seems more akin to the laws for the protection of nonhumans of many European countries, mentioned above.

Also, in this case, the law is based on the theory of indirect duties, since nonhumans do not rise to the status of persons, or of legal entities. In contrast

to what is stipulated in the Treaty of Lisbon, there is no theoretical reference
to the elevation of animals from the condition of objects to that of subjects.

With the use of the term "protection" is implicit adhesion to welfarism.
However, confirmed by the type of system, which, while referring to the
importance of biodiversity and the preservation of wildlife, does not contain
any reference to the relevance of the individuals as right-holders.

Some constitutional experts have expressed skepticism about the possibility of including animal rights in the Constitution:

> The compression of human rights by the Constitution may happen only if it is
> necessary to the realization of other human rights or public interests, related to
> the first. With a joke, believe that constitutionalism is incompatible with the
> rodent as a measure violated the right to life of the mice, it would be a
> laughable assertion that no lawyer would even dare to move forward. It must
> therefore be concluded that the constitutionalism leads to the configuration of
> animal rights, but not in terms that could lead to constitutional status of equal-
> ity between humans and other species. [75]

The Swiss choice appears to reveal substantial similarities with the Italian
constitutional bill no. 4429/03. In both cases animals are considered as members of the ecosystem, rather than as individuals; on the other hand, while the
Italian proposal makes express reference to the right of future generations,
the Swiss constitution does not go so far as to identify the foundation (and
thus the *ratio legis*).

The transposition in the constitution of nonhuman animals, by itself, does
not imply the granting of any right, nor the legal subjectivity; as it was found
from the comparison to Italian proposals and foreign legal systems, there are
several roads likely to include animals in the Constitution.

The main differences between the choices above are clear at this point:
the two main currents, opposite each other, are that of the protection of
animals for themselves and that, antithetical, of animals as part of the ecosystem and/or in the interest of humans (eventually referring to future generations).

The experiences, however brief, of the Swiss constitution, as well as the
German one, show that there is no direct predetermined link between nor the
attribution of constitutional importance to nonhuman and legislative inter-
ventions; probably, both institutions go hand in hand, receiving and transfer-
ring the right in the social feeling.

For now it seems that the constitutionalization of animal issues plays a
role eminently ideological and principled, while it would be difficult to argue
that this is necessary in order to achieve a complete legal protection, as the
comparative study of laws does not lead to recognizing particular differences
among Western countries that have made different choices in this regard.

The Italian Proposals

The Italian Constitution is already used, by interpretation, to protect the environment, as its article no. 9 recits: "*The Republic promotes the development of culture and scientific and technical research. It protects the landscape and the historical and artistic heritage of the Nation.*" The following statement was added to paragraph II: "*Nonhuman animal species have an equal right to life and a life compatible with their biological characteristics. The Republic recognizes all animals as subjects of law. It promotes and develops services and initiatives to respect animals and the protection of their dignity and punish any attack on their existence.*"[76]

The above formulation does not include animals, while many animal advocates consider it possible to amend such provision to insert animal rights in the Italian Constitution; the first attempt was on March 18, 1998, when Congresswoman Anna Maria Procacci filed bill no. 4690. In the memorandum that accompanied the parliamentary act, we read: "*Who, indeed, are animals? They are food, friends, pests, disease-carrying, means of work, source of aesthetic enjoyment, means of entertainment, resources 'renewable,' food producers, predators, object of research for therapists, sources of raw materials, and more.*"

The first reference to the relationship between man and animal concerns precisely eating (animal = food). It is clear the intention of the legislature to affect this phenomenon, ensuring that the right of an individual (human) ends where that of any nonhuman animal begins.

Still, the preamble states that:

> The society has recognized the need to protect especially the most vulnerable individuals. So the common sentiment is addressed to protect them more, due to the objective difficulty stating their rights. If this perspective is considered to be significant, it is legitimate to extend it to any holder of rights, regardless of the group, race, or species to which they belong.

Implicit is the reference to *antispeciesism*. Given the lack of means of self-protection by nonhuman animals, humans would have the duty of preparing the same legislative framework of protection that has been given to minorities and to the most vulnerable or disadvantaged persons throughout history.

The constitutional principle that the proposed amendment refers to is that of solidarity, which is already accepted in article 2 of the Constitution, which refers to "*fundamental human rights.*"

The grounds on which it is considered appropriate to include *sub* art. 9 the protection of animals are descended primarily from the interpretation of case law, which, over the years, has extended the application of the rule, to encompass ecology and environment.

On the basis of the above, with the judgments nos. 151 and 153, in 1986, the Constitutional Court ruled that the environment represents a value of fundamental importance and that has, in fact, constitutional relevance; in this, animals would then be considered as a natural extension of the concept of environment, nature, and ecosystem.

The draft of Constitutional Law no. 4429, presented on October 28, 2003 at the Parliament, is an example of the instances of reform of article 9 ecologically oriented. In this formulation, in fact, there is no express reference to animals, but to "*the defense of biodiversity, the balance of ecosystems and hydrological cycles, which are considered common property of mankind.*"[77]

In a different perspective lie the other proposals for amendment of art. 9 of the Constitution that have been formulated over the last fifteen years and that are based on considerations of environment as indirect human interest.

Therefore, the Constitutional Law amendment mentioned above at the same time intends to recognize nonhuman animals and to protect their dignity, with respect to any interference by humans, through the adoption of all appropriate measures to recognize their intrinsic value.

The US Proposals

The US Bill of Rights, unlike many European Constitutions, is very short and general, and it is mainly dedicated to human freedoms; unlike the Italian proposals to reform one or more provisions of the existing Constitution, the US proposals suggest the adoption of a brand new Bill of Rights, entirely dedicated to animals.

An effort to enforce animal rights at a constitutional level in the US is that of the Animal Legal Defense Fund that made the proposal of an Animal Bill of Rights.[78]

The Bill is articulated in six amendments, as follows:

1. *The right of animals to be free from exploitation, cruelty, neglect, and abuse.*
2. *The right of laboratory animals to not be used in cruel or unnecessary experiments.*
3. *The right of companion animals to a healthy diet, protective shelter, and adequate medical care.*
4. *The right of wildlife to a natural habitat, ecologically sufficient to a normal existence and self-sustaining population.*
5. *The right of farmed animals to an environment that satisfies their basic physical and psychological needs.*
6. *The right of animals to have their interest represented in court and safeguarded by the law of the land.*

Like some of the Italian proposals, that in the United States is also based on the will of animal advocates to elevate the protection rank of animals from the law to a constitutional level; the structure shows its similarity with the welfare laws, which does not imply the end of animal exploitation, but rather its regulation.

Even in this case, the main question might be not *if* such a proposal will be accepted, but *what would change* in the case that they are approved. We have seen that in those Western countries where the animal interests have been recognized at a Constitutional level, nothing has changed practically; is there anything in the American proposal that may lead to a different conclusion?

After this short analysis, we can conclude that, in the present, the fact that a Constitution includes animals at any level does not actually make any difference in their condition, nor in the human duties toward animals.

Although a constitutional reform might be useless today, it is possible to consider that it could represent the basis for wider legal reforms in the near future, according to the change in the common feeling.

NOTES

1. Jellamo, Anna, *Il cammino di Dike – L'idea di giustizia da Omero a Eschilo*, Donzelli Editore, Roma, 2005, p. 35.

2. Sanfilippo, *Istituzioni di diritto romano*, X edizione, Rubbettino Editore, Catanzaro, 2002, p. 41.

3. Cerutti, *Giustizia sommaria*, Feltrinelli, Milano, 2003, p. 89.

4. Onida, *Studi sulla condizione degli animali non umani nel sistema giuridico romano*, Giappichelli, Torino, 2002, p. 499.

5. Ibid., p. 198.

6. *Res mancipi* are things that may be yield by *mancipatio*, distinguished by *res nec mancipi*, that requie just the *traditio*.

7. Ferrara, Morena, Felici, Guaria, *Guida alla prevenzione e repressione dei maltrattamenti agli animali*, Maggioli Editore, Sant'Arcangelo di Romagna, 2012, p. 32.

8. See Rescigno and Onida.

9. See Italian Civil Code, article no. 925.

10. Bordon, Raniero, Rossi, Stefano, Tramontano, Luigi, *La nuova responsabilità civile. Casualità. Responsabilità oggettiva. Lavoro*, UTET Giuridica, Torino, 2002, p. 533.

11. In any case, the owner is exempted from liability for damages, by alienating the animal to the injured party.

12. Ulpian, *Digest*, 9.1.1.3: *"Pauperies est damnum sine iniuria facientis datum: nec enim potest animal iniuria fecisse quod sensu caret."*

13. La Torre, *Cinquant'anni col diritto*, Giuffrè Editore, Milano, 2008, p. 210.

14. Ulp., 19.5.14.3.

15. This means the animals associated with the cultivation and breeding: horses, cattle, and pigs.

16. If, for example, a mule had kicked for being conducted on a particularly steep hill or was excessively loaded compared to its capacity, this is considered liability in tort, due to the negligence or carelessness of the owner.

17. Ulp., 21.1.42: *"Qua vulgo iter fiet, ita habuisse velit, ut cuiquam nocere damnumve dare possit, si adversus ea factum erit et homo liber ex ea re perierit, solidi ducenti, si nocitum*

homini libero esse dicetur, quanti bonum aequum iudici videbitur, condemnetur, ceterarum rerum, quanti damnum datum factumve sit, dupli."

18. Giust., Digest (9, 2, 2)*: Lege Aquilia capite primo cavetur: "si quis servum servamve alienum alienamve quadrupedem vel pecudem iniuria occiderit, quanti id in eo anno plurimi fuit, tantum aes dare domino damnas esto.*"

19. Galgano, *Trattato di diritto civile: gli atti unilaterali e i titoli di credito*, Wolters Kluwer, Milano, 2010, p. 115.

20. Ferrara, *Visioni storico-filosofiche e fonti della tutela giuridica degli animali*, in: Ferrara, Morena, Felici, Guaria, p. 30.

21. See *supra*, p. 55.

22. According to Roman law, people could be born slaves, or become such by conquest (military) or for unpaid debts.

23. Falcòn Y Tella, J. M., Falcòn Y Tella, F., *Fondamento e finalità della sanzione: diritto di punire?* Giuffrè, Milano, 2008, p. 87.

24. Ibid.

25. Castignone, *La questione animale*, in Rodotà, S., Tallacchini, M., *Ambito e fonti del biodiritto*, in *Trattato di biodiritto*, Giuffrè, Milano, 2010, p. 22.

26. Kojève, Alexandre, *Linee di una fenomenologia del diritto*, Jaca Book, Milano, 1989, p. 43.

27. Not so with regard to humans, who, in the meantime, had been emancipated from slavery because of the cultural, economic, social, and technological.

28. Mannucci, *Animali e diritto italiano: una storia*, Jan. 2004, http://www.google.com/url?sa=t&rct=j&q=&esrc=s&source=web&cd=1&cts=1331564192999&ved=0CCYQFjAA&url=http%3A%2F%2Fwww.olir.it%2Fareetematiche%2F42%2Fdocuments%2Fmannucci_ani maliediritto.pdf&ei=ng5eT5_ON6Wi0QXhrsTfDQ&usg=AFQjCNH7x7d_ZDioIj1YRF7UiGSbO9bJQw&sig2=PQr3dAVNQ02FnX9joae0Hg

29. http://en.wikisource.org/wiki/Martin's_Act_1822.

30. http://www.animalrightshistory.org/animal-rights-law/romantic-legislation/1822-uk-act-ill-treatment-cattle.htm. The first article says: "*Whereas it is expedient to prevent the cruel and improper Treatment of Horses, Mares, Geldings, Mules, Asses, Cows, Heifers, Steers, Oxen, Sheep, and other Cattle: May it therefore please Your Majesty, by and with the Advice and Consent of the Lords Spiritual and Temporal, and Commons, in this present Parliament assembled, and by the Authority of the same, That if any person or persons shall wantonly and cruelly beat, abuse, or ill-treat any Horse, Mare, Gelding, Mule, Ass, Ox, Cow, Heifer, Steer, Sheep, or other Cattle, and Complaint on Oath thereof be made to any Justice of the Peace or other Magistrate within whose Jurisdiction such Offence shall be committed, it shall be lawful for such Justice of the Peace or other Magistrate to issue his Summons or Warrant, at his Discretion, to bring the party or parties so complained of before him, or any other Justice of the Peace or other Magistrate of the County, City, or place within which such Justice of the Peace or other Magistrate has Jurisdiction, who shall examine upon Oath any Witness or Witnesses who shall appear or be produced to give Information touching such Offence, (which Oath the said Justice of the Peace or other Magistrate is hereby authorized and required to administer); and if the party or parties accused shall be convicted of any such Offence, either by his, her, or their own Confession, or upon such Information as aforesaid, he, she, or they so convicted shall forfeit and pay any Sum not exceeding Five Pounds, not less than Ten Shillings, to His Majesty, His Heirs and Successors; and if the person or persons so convicted shall refuse or not be able forthwith to pay the Sum forfeited, every such Offender shall, by Warrant under the Hand and Seal of some Justice or Justices of the Peace or other Magistrate within whose Jurisdiction the person offending shall be Convicted, be committed to the House of Correction or some other Prison within the Jurisdiction within which the Offence shall have been committed, there to be kept without Bail or Main prize for any Time not exceeding Three Months.*"

31. See *supra*, § 1.4.

32. http://www.animalrightshistory.org/animal-rights-law/romantic-legislation/1835-uk-act-cruelty-to-animals.htm

33. http://webcache.googleusercontent.com/
search?q=cache:kUc6tlGNKeIJ:www.italgiure.giustizia.it/nir/lexs/1977/lexs _25 8897.html+&
cd=1&hl=it&ct=clnk

34. See Cass. Pen., sent. 28/10/82.

35. See D. Lgs. 267/00, article no. 19

36. See Cass. Civ. Sez. III, no. 23095/10 and no. 80/10.

37. Also stray pets are considered wildlife.

38. Sgrò, Renato Maria, *Sulle fonti dell'art. 727 del codice penale*, in Castignone – Battaglia, *I diritti degli animali*, Centro di bioetica di Genova, 1987, p. 61.

39. Cadoppi, *Trattato di diritto penale - Parte speciale Vol. VI: Delitti contro la moralità pubblica, di prostituzione, contro il sentimento per gli animali e contro la famiglia*, UTET Giuridica, Torino, 2010, p. 95.

40. Mannucci, *Animali e diritto italiano: una storia*, in *Per un codice degli animali*, Giuffrè, Milano, 2001, p. 9.

41. http://www.anpana.puglia.it/files/l611-13_provvedimen-
ti_per_la_protezione_degli_ani.pdf

42. Fiandaca, *Prospettive possibili di maggiore tutela penale degli animali*, in *Per un codice degli animali*, Giuffrè, Milano, 2001.

43. See *supra*, § 1.4.

44. http://www.camera.it/parlam/leggi/04189l.htm

45. See *supra*, § 1.1.

46. See *supra*, § 1.1, nota n. 29.

47. Italian law dismissed the concept of *lex naturalis*, avoiding any term corresponding to it.

48. See *supra*, § 1.2.

49. http://www.salute.gov.it/imgs/C_17_normativa_925_allegato.pdf

50. http://www.repubblica.it/online/cultura_scienze/mucca/pazza/pazza.html

51. http://www.salute.gov.it/imgs/C_17_pagineAree_1558_listaFile_itemName_6_file.pdf

52. http://www.salute.gov.it/imgs/C_17_normativa_911_allegato.pdf

53. See *supra*, § 1.4.

54. http://www.normativasanitaria.it/jsp/dettaglio.jsp?aggiornamenti=&id=26262&page=&
posArt=1&articolo=1&subart =1&progr=1&anno=null

55. http://conventions.coe.int/Treaty/ita/Treaties/Html/102.htm

56. http://www.consilium.europa.eu/treaty-of-lisbon?lang=it.

57. Grassi, Stefano, *La tutela degli animali nella prospettiva della "tutela dell'ambiente e dell'ecosistema"*, in *Trattato di biodiritto. La questione Animale*, p. 317.

58. See art. 1, Ordinance of Labor, Health and Social Politics Minister 16 July 2009.

59. Pisanò, p. 84.

60. http://www.legifrance.gouv.fr/affich-
Code.do;jsessionid=8460B46254C1EF9B9F76DECE7BF307D3.tpdjo17v_3?idS   ection-
TA=LEGISCTA000006149860&cidTexte=LEGITEXT000006070719&dateTexte=20120313

61. http://abogadospenal.fullblog.com.ar/codigo-penal-espanol---texto-integro-actualizado-
2-121244071996.html

62. See *"The agricolture (miscellaneous provisions) act"* (1968) and*"Animals (scientific procedures) act"* (1986).

63. http://www.legislation.gov.uk/ukpga/Geo5/1-2/27

64. See section no. 11: *"If the owner is absent or refuses to consent to the destruction of the animal [...] it shall be lawful for the police constable, without the consent of the owner, to slaughter the animal."*

65. http://www.gesetze-im-internet.de/tierschg/BJNR012770972.html

66. http://www.gpo.gov/fdsys/pkg/USCODE-2009-title7/pdf/USCODE-2009-title7-
chap54.pdf

67. http://www.gpo.gov/fdsys/pkg/CFR-2009-title9-vol1/pdf/CFR-2009-title9-vol1-chapI-
subchapA.pdf

68. http://frwebgate.access.gpo.gov/cgibin/usc.cgi?ACTION=RETRIEVE&
FILE=$$xa$$busc7.wais&start=6283691&SI ZE=5930&TYPE=TEXT

69. http://aldf.org/downloads/APL6E-CA.pdf

70. Regan and Francione denied that killing animals for food may be justified by need, stating that there is not any kind of need connected with eating meat, while Western laws seems to consider it as a need.

71. Gemma, *Costituzione   e   tutela   degli   animali*,   27/4/04,   articolo: http://www.forumcostituzionale.it/site/images/stories/pdf/old_pdf/803.pdf

72. See *supra*, § 1.1.

73. This was not a binding rule, and, therefore, it has to be considered just as a sort of reminder that the European Community directed to its countries. It was not directly enforceable by any citizen of those countries.

74. See *supra*, § 2.2.

75. Gemma, *Costituzione   e   tutela   degli   animali*,   27/4/04,   articolo: http://www.forumcostituzionale.it/site/images/stories/pdf/old_pdf/803.pdf

76. http://legislature.camera.it/_dati/leg13/lavori/stampati/sk5000/articola/4690.htm

77. http://legxiv.camera.it/_dati/leg14/lavori/stampati/sk4500/articola/4429.htm

78. http://animalbillofrights.aldf.org/

Chapter Three

Nonhumans Right to Life and Vegetarianism in Positive Law

3.1 THE CASE LAW

All the animal advocates who are philosophers, whether or not they claimed the recognition of real rights for nonhumans, agree on the food issue, considering a vegetarian/vegan diet as an imperative, while our laws are just beginning to face such matters.

Vegetarianism/veganism involves a multitude of social and legal relations, as well as the interests of individuals and those of associations, societies, institutions, etc.; the case law are consequently very heterogeneous.

In the Western world the legal issues about vegetarianism that culminated in court so far have focused mainly on two types of relations:

- parents and children;
- buyer-seller.

Questions of the first type often descend from the disagreement between parents about the common feeding of children, or from external complaints about the adequacy of their nutrition.

Cases of the second type are widespread in the restoration business and can be ascribed to faulty or willful misconduct. In both cases, the dispute arises from the omission, or erroneous or unsuitable information about the products featured in the dishes offered for consumption.

The Suspension of Parental Authority for Vegetarian Parents

A well-discussed case occurred in Milan in 1999, when Chiara, a one-year-old baby, was brought by her parents to the emergency room for respiratory problems. The doctors of the structure, having considered the baby under conditions of malnutrition, decided to keep her for investigations and treatments, also highlighting the case to the Juvenile Court of Milan.[1]

The judge decided that the parents were not fulfilling their obligations, bearing also serious damage to the child's health; on the basis of these considerations, therefore, the child was put under the custody of the Municipality of Milan, with the suspension of any parental rights.

Of course, the Court's decision was highly publicized, and it sharpened the contrast between proponents and opponents of vegetarianism, and, in legal terms, about assumptions and opportunity of the pronunciation.

Dr. Livia Pomodoro, then president of the Juvenile Court of Milan, defended the decision, stating: *"We always respect the choices, but we cannot intervene when there is dancing in the right to health [...] C ' is a parental responsibility, but not a right to life or death to the child."*

The debate from the courtroom soon moved to the media and was attended by doctors and nutritionists from both parties—the first to support the correctness of the judges, the latter, on the contrary, to contest it.

Doctors opposed to the parental choices stated that:

> The so-called vegans whose name derives from Vegan, the Englishman who was the initiator of this philosophy of food; his followers exclude from their diet any animal food, including milk and eggs. Despite being aware that eggs and milk cannot be considered strictly 'animals,' they exclude them anyway because their production causes suffering to animals themselves [...] You can live well eating vegetarian, without risk to health. Plant proteins are more than sufficient for the needs of a human organism. For someone who eats too many eggs or cheese too, there may be a risk of an excessive consumption of saturated fats. [...] When a population is accustomed to eating little and following a vegetarian diet, it's bad when it suddenly begins to eat protein foods, which Westerners have become accustomed to [...] Personally, I think that the ideal diet is fish-vegetarian diet, based on plants and fish, with the addition of yogurt.[2]

The same nutritionist, after explaining the above and warning against the consumption of foods of animal origin, said: *"Before two years of age, the vegetarian diet, especially if in the strict sense, is absolutely not recommended. After weaning, children become omnivores, but have to supplement their diet with milk."*[3]

Giorgio Calabrese, a famous nutritionist, speaking against the choice of vegetarian parents, said:

The vegetarian diet that these two parents followed already in first person is totally unbalanced for their child [...] because it lacks proteins resulting primarily from foods of animal origin and at the same time lacks Vitamin B12 and Folic Acid, Calcium, Vitamin D, Vitamin B2, and iodine. The first two elements are essential for the balance of the production of red blood cells and to make them work well, avoiding severe anemia and preventing damage to the nervous tissue. Calcium is essential for the integrity and the formation of bones and teeth, both in the mother nurse, both in children and is also used for the proper functioning of muscles, including the heart and nervous system. Vitamin D helps to prevent rickets in children; Vitamin B2, whose deficiency can cause damage to the skin, especially around the nose and mouth and can give eye disorders. Iodine balances the thyroid that, if altered, causes so many troubles that it is better to avoid.[4]

Dr. Riccardo Trespidi, supporting the vegetarian diet, also for infants and children, argued:

It is scientifically proven that a vegetarian diet is recommended, as it helps to reduce certain diseases such as cancer, high blood pressure, obesity. [...] Eating vegetarian, in a proper way, means health. This is also true for infants: if breast milk is not available, there is soy milk. At weaning, add vegetable purees supplemented with barley, rice, or millet. And a lot of fruit. Following this regime, the kids are fine. I hope that the judges will intervene to terminate the parental rights also to the parents who give their children snacks and burgers, until they become obese.[5]

From a legal perspective, the matter shall focus on the protection of the right to health, and, therefore, on the way to ensure it. The medical, scientific, and historical documentation, now part of the Western cultural heritage, do not consider vegetarianism and veganism deleterious to health, but the opposite. The Milan case resulted in the mistaken attribution of the child's illness to the vegetarian diet, while, if anything, the problem consisted in malnutrition, which can occur both in omnivorous and vegetarian/vegan diets.

What has emerged seems to be the erroneous classification of the problem, which led to the wrong conclusion to change the dietary pattern, rather than correcting that already adopted; as many suggested, in short, the decision of the Court should have taken into consideration the parents' ethical instances, by ensuring the compliance with those measures that the Court deemed as the most appropriate for the child's health (hospitalization, therapy, etc.).

After the aforesaid case in Milan, there was a similar case in Lecce (Southern Italy), where the Court relieved the parental rights of a vegetarian couple whose two-year-old daughter was entrusted to a religious institution, while the parental visits were permitted after the intervention of social services, aimed at "re-education." The couple was only able to regain custody of the child after about a year.[6]

The principle underlying such pronunciations is *Vegetarianism = lesion of children's right to health*, hence the adoption of all remedies consequential and, in particular, social service's custody or limitation of parental authority.

The delicacy of the abovementioned issues concerns not only the law, but inevitably pertains to science and nutrition. The decision on the subject, even if based on assertions made by the judge's expert, is evidently not without controversy, given the coexistence of different orientations among scientists and therapists about nutrition.

A similar case occurred in England, where, in March 2008, a six-year-old child had a sudden collapse and was rushed to the hospital, where the doctors diagnosed—among other things—a form of rickets, which they considered due to the vegan choice made by his parents.

The couple claimed to have three more children in good health, emphasizing the need to not practice vegetarianism, but also to eat fish, though excluding milk and meat. Nevertheless, social services forced hospitalization for about six months, during which the parents could visit the child only under the supervision of qualified personnel. Meanwhile, the City Council took legal action to obtain the child's custody, taking him away from the family. In this case, however, the judge ruled in favor of the parents, ordering the return of the child and periodic inspections by doctors.[7]

Apart from the considerations in the merits of the case and the purely medical aspects, the English Court's decision, unlike the Italian case, has also expressed apprehension toward parental relationships and parental choices, combining them with the child's protection, acknowledging the scientific information in the matter, and, thus, confirming the view that the absence of meat and milk does not cause any injury to health.

In the England case the fact that vegetarianism/veganism is more historically grounded than in Italy seems relevant, and that, consequently, the social perception of non-value with respect to this choice is attenuated.

A similar question has recently risen to prominence in the news from the island of Crete, in Greece, where a vegetarian couple decided to apply for the adoption of a child and has been refused because of their vegetarian diet.

The social services that made the controversial decision justified it by saying that they were based on an authoritative opinion, provided by the University of Medicine in Crete, according to which children need to eat *"meat and fish."*[8]

Professor Antonis Kafatos, author of the abovementioned opinion, called such a decision to deny the adoption *"unreasonable,"* based on the choice of candidates vegetarian parents, stating that meat is not essential for growth.

In another case, involving Italy and Germany, parents disputed for custody of their child, and the mother alleged that the vegetarian diet practiced by the father was not suitable for their daughter. The child's father, a vegetarian German citizen, obtained custody of his daughter from the German Court. The foreign judgment, approved and therefore made effective in Italy, was flatly rejected by the child's mother, who kept the girl with her in Tuscany.

The child's mother said that her daughter would have suffered from malnutrition due to the father's vegetarian choice, and that, therefore, she would not have consented to leave.[9]

The legal battle, which took place in Germany, ruled in favor of the father this time, and dismissed the view that a vegetarian diet would endanger the health or growth of the child. [10]

Legal aspects involved in these events are essentially two, both of constitutional status: freedom of thought and manifestation of personality on the one hand, and the right to health on the other; often, the conflict is based on the assumption that the two rights are opposed, to determine whether the right to raise children as vegetarians should prevail, or the respect for their health.

Legal defense of parents who are having their right to choose a vegetarian/vegan diet for their children contested might naturally consider both issues: the right to free expression of thought and, therefore, the education of children, and also medical aspects underlying vegetarianism/veganism. Anyway, a preliminary observation is fundamental. This opposition stems from the assumption that eating meat is beneficial and vegetarianism harmful, but what if that is not the case, or if the roles were reversed?

The core of any defense will inevitably take into account the medic-scientific aspects of eating, having to provide full proof to the judge that vegetarianism/veganism is not only a legitimate alternative, but even healthier if compared to the consumption of animal products, even (especially) in childhood.

Once the defense has demonstrated the equivalence between different diets, or even the superiority of vegetarianism/veganism, facing different questions would be superfluous.

It often happens that the judge, or at least the counterpart, consider the vegetarian/vegan choice as an improper imposition over children—this argument is clearly ungrounded, as parents always have to make a choice for their children (not only about food), both omnivores and vegetarians.

Block v. McDonald's

The second kind of questions involves commercial relations (particularly restoration) very common in everyday life.

One of the main issues that involve vegetarian/vegan consumers is the non-disclosure or wrong indication of food ingredients.

The identification of ingredients is crucial—especially when they are sub-tle, hidden, or present in very small amounts—for a vegetarian to be sure not to eat animal products when consuming food outside their home.

A precedent of major importance is the controversy that involved the giant McDonald's in the early 2000s, when they were accused by consumers of spreading misleading advertising regarding the presence or absence of animal products in some dishes.

On July 23rd, 1990, McDonald's sent out a press release stating that its french fries were fried in 100% vegetable oils.

In 2001 the American writer Eric Schlosser published a book entitled *Fast Food Nation*, in which he reported, among other things, that the ingre-dients listed as "natural flavors" in french fries at McDonald's actually con-tained beef, used in the oil used to pre-fry potatoes in processing plants.[11] The information was confirmed on April 6th, 2001, by the same public relations officers of the company, who responded positively to the request that a consumer submitted via e-mail.

On June 6th, 2001, Haris Bharti, an American lawyer of Indian origin, launched a class action lawsuit against McDonald's to obtain compensation for the damage caused to the customers on the basis of the above; the case is known as *Block v. McDonald's Corporation*.

The first McDonald's reaction was to deny the previous statement that dates back to 1990, stating that french fries were never indicated as vegetar-ian, and, hence, adding that the indication of *natural flavoring* in reference to the extract of beef was legal.

In the meanwhile, it was discovered that in other cases the company had promoted its french fries as vegetarian, for example, in a letter written in 1993 by an employee of the company, in which he listed the dishes suitable for vegetarians, including french fries.

The judge in charge, Richard Siebel, recognizing the precariousness of the procedural status of the actor, informed that it would be "*difficult to prove liability on the merits*."[12]

Despite the above, the fast food giant had already received significant negative publicity, which in some cases had even led to violent demonstra-tions, as happened in India, where the company had to clarify that it had never distributed fried potatoes enriched with beef in that area of the world.

At the end, the fear of losing the lawsuit on the one hand and to receive further image damage on the other hand led the parties to a settlement agree-ment, signed on April 26th, 2002, providing for the payment by McDonald's of an amount equal to $10,000,000, of which $6,000,000 would be allocated to vegetarian societies/movements.

Moreover, it is interesting to note that even in 2011, the corporation had not changed its recipes, so as to confirm to use potatoes pre-fried in oil containing added beef, while specifying that such information relates to the American market.[13]

The class action included the following categories of persons:

> Who: (i) have consumed french fries or hash browns from or at McDonald's restaurants in the United States since July 23, 1990; and (ii) have concerns, objections or dietary restrictions, whether ethical, moral, religious, philosophical, or health-related, with respect to the consumption of beef or meat." The foundation of the claims was deduced: "Violations of the consumer fraud laws and common law principles of all 50 states. The Action alleges that McDonald's provided false and misleading nutritional information to consumers by failing to disclose that its french fries and hash browns contain a small amount of beef flavoring and thus are not vegetarian.[14]

In short, according to the plaintiffs, McDonald's had been guilty of fraud and unfair trade practices, through the false indication of nutritional information, by failing to declare that their french fries contained meat and that they were, therefore, not vegetarian.

The writ of summons concluded that:

> As a proximate result of the defendant's wrongful conduct, plaintiffs and the class members have sustained damages. Defendant's conduct was intentionally fraudulent, warranting substantial punitive damages.
>
> "WHEREFORE, plaintiffs request that the Court enter judgment in favor of plaintiffs and the class and against defendant for:
>
> "Actual and punitive damages;
>
> "An injunction restraining future nondisclosures;
>
> "Restitution, disgorgement, and other equitable monetary relief;
>
> "Attorney's fees, litigation expenses, and costs of suit.[15]

The fraudulent nature, which the Italian legal system defines *"mala fede"* or "malicious" (even with criminal relevance), in American law legitimates the conviction to pay punitive damages, which are a form of penalty consisting in the payment of a sum additional to that due to the damage actually caused and quantified.

The epilogue of the story was the settlement agreement, where McDonald's agreed to make:

1. the donation of $10,000,000 in favor of non-profit organizations involving: Vegetarianism (60%), Hindu or Sikh (20%), child nutrition funds or food for children (10%), promotion and dissemination of Kosher Jewish practice (10%);
2. the publication of a formal apology;
3. the adoption of a detailed schedule of each type of vegetarian dietary restrictions and guidelines for companies that cater to vegetarians;

4. the payment of $ 4,000 in favor of each of the twelve actors;
5. the payment of legal fees, including fees of $ 2,452,000 for the de-
   fenders of the actors.[16]

Gupta v. Asha Enterprises LLC

On August 10th, 2009 Mr. Durges Gupta, a Hindu American citizen, went
with a friend to buy some takeaway meals for themselves and other friends,
at the chain restaurant Moghul Express. He and his friend specifically asked
if samosa contained meat, claiming to be vegetarians, and the attendant told
them that the restaurant did not sell any kind of samosa with meat. Only later,
once they had started eating, did Gupta and his friends find the presence of
meat, later also confirmed by the restaurant staff, which is why customers
have decided to take legal action alleging *"negligence, negligent infliction of
emotional distress, consumer fraud, product liability, and breach of express
and implied warranties."*[17]

The claims are partly similar to those of Block v. McDonald's, where
commercial fraud was also claimed, but this has added a number of claims
related to personal injury.

While McDonald's was asked to pay damages (including punitive) that
consisted of having led to the purchase of a product without the promised
features (dishes of potatoes not vegetarian, advertised as such), in the case of
Gupta v. Asha Enterprises LLC the claim was intended to obtain compensation for the emotional suffering that the accidental ingestion of meat caused
to the plaintiffs, as well as the cost of the remedy.

According to Hindu tradition, after the ingestion of meat it is necessary to
be purified by immersing in the Ganges, and, therefore, in addition to nonpe-
cuniary damage, Gupta claimed the price of the entire trip from the USA to
India.

A State Trial Court dismissed all of the plaintiffs' claims, stating that it
could not find any basis in accordance with NJPLA (New Jersey Products
Liability Act), not being able to recognize any inherent defect in the product
provided by the restaurant. Plaintiffs, however, decided to appeal the decision, and the New Jersey Appellate ruled on July 18, 2011 with the following
verdict: *"Affirmed in part, reversed in part and remanded."*[18]

The Appellate Court considered all of the plaintiffs' arguments, starting
from the alleged unsuitability of the product under NJPLA (NJSA 2A: 58C-1
to -11), which states:

> A manufacturer or seller of a product shall be liable in a product liability
> action only if the claimant proves by a preponderance of the evidence that the
> product causing the harm was not reasonably fit, suitable, or safe for its in-
> tended purpose because it: a. deviated from the design specifications, formu-
> lae, or performance standards of the manufacturer or from otherwise identical

units manufactured to the same manufacturing specifications or formulae, or b. failed to contain adequate warnings or instructions, or c. was designed in a defective manner.

In short, the rule invoked by the plaintiffs involves only defect or lack of conformity or design of the product, while such circumstances did not occur in the food administered and that, instead, appeared different from that stated but not defective or unsuitable to the intended purpose (in this case eating).

On the basis of the above, the Appellate Court stated: "*The PLA is inapplicable as grounds for recovery in the present case because plaintiffs' claims are not related to a defect in the samosas themselves, which were safe, edible, and fit for human consumption, but rather to allegations that they were supplied the wrong product.*"

Therefore, the Appellate Court confirmed the judgment under appeal in so far as the State Court did not consider applicable the above-mentioned rule, insisting that the plaintiffs' demand based on such argument could not be accepted. The other claims were approved, including that based on the New Jersey Consumer Fraud Act, which states:

> The act, use, or employment by any person of any unconscionable commercial practice, deception, fraud, false pretense, false promise, misrepresentation, or the knowing [...] concealment, suppression, or omission of any material fact with intent that others rely upon such concealment, suppression, or omission, in connection with the sale or advertisement of any merchandise ... whether or not any person has in fact been misled, deceived or damaged thereby, is declared to be an unlawful practice. (NJSA 56:8-2)

About that the Appellate Court found decisive the fact that the restaurant's staff had assured the client that there was no meat in the samosa, in addition to the fact that it was labeled as "*VEG Samosa.*"

As for moral damages allegedly caused by the negligent conduct of the caterer, the Appellate Court upheld the decision of the State Court, stating that such recognition would have led to the establishment of new laws for the protection of eating choices of each religion; against such interpretation, anyway, the Appellate Court argued that the real limit of that claim is the principle of foreseeability of the damage, which this case lacked.

Finally, the Appellate Court focused on the claims based on the guarantee of the seller disciplined by UCC (Uniform Commercial Code), which considers binding:

> (a) Any affirmation of fact or promise made by the seller to the buyer which relates to the goods and becomes part of the basis of the bargain creates an express warranty that the goods shall conform to the affirmation or promise;
> (b) Any description of the goods which is made part of the basis of the bargain creates an express warranty that the goods shall conform to the description.

The Appellate Court accepted the existence of the plaintiffs' *prima facie* evidence in relation to the warranty provided by the seller and, more precisely, voiced through the reassurances of the catering staff; skepticism, however, has been expressed about the opportunity to receive an amount of expenses for travel in India cathartic purpose; according to the Court, this would require evidence of predictability by the restaurateur.

While the case was pending, that following the Appellate Court's decision was remitted to the State Court, certain principles have already been established (or confirmed): the attribution of characteristics false or omitted statement of the real ones is an unfair business practice and, as such, requires the author to pay compensation for the damage caused.

Likewise, sellers are obliged to pay compensation when they ingenerate an expectation into the buyer, through the guarantee of quality that the product does not actually offer. These issues are linked by the discrepancy between what is proposed and what is provided. The difference between the two cases stems from the fact that in one case it configures misleading advertising, which, as such, is illegal and makes the seller liable regardless of any damage caused, while, in the other case, the claim arises from the existence of a contractual relationship between the parties and the evidence of consequential damages suffered by the purchaser due to false promises of the seller.

Nelissa Adelpour and Kevin Shenkman, et al. V. Panda Express, Inc., et al. Shenkman and v. Chipotle Mexican Grill Inc.

Almost simultaneously with the lawsuit filed in New Jersey, two other similar cases occurred in California, where the vegetarian lawyer Kevin Shenkman sued the restaurant chains Chipotle and Panda Express. At first, in fact, he was served the "pinto beans" with the addition of bacon, while in the second restaurant he claims to have discovered the use of chicken powder in various allegedly vegetarian dishes.[19]

In the case *Nelissa Adelpour and Kevin Shenkman, et al. V. Panda Express, Inc., etc. al.*, filed on November 12, 2009, a class action lawsuit was promoted against the restaurant chain, including

> "All California residents who abstain from consuming animal flesh or animal products for any reasons such as dietary restrictions, religious beliefs, or ethical reasons, and who purchased the food products 'Steamed Veggies,' 'Eggplant & Tofu,' 'String Beans with Tofu,' 'Sauteed String Beans,' 'Vegetable Fried Rice,' or 'Vegetable Chow Mein' at or from a Panda Express restaurant located in the state of California at any time during the four years preceding the filing of the Complaint to class certification (the 'Vegetarian Class')"[20] ,

namely all the vegetarians who consumed the food allegedly meatless, which actually contained chicken powder.

Subsequently, on March 2nd, 2010, the plaintiffs changed the classes, adding a second one:

> "All California residents who purchased vegetarian or meat-free dishes and purchased the Subject Food Products at or from a Panda Express restaurant located in the state of California at any time during the period of four years preceding the filing of the Complaint to class certification (the 'Defrauded Class')," namely all the users who had bought food on the basis of a wrong description.

Also in the case *Shenkman v. Chipotle Mexican Grill Inc.* the judicial initiative took the form of a class action on behalf of all the citizens of California who reject the consumption of pork or bacon and who bought pinto beans at Chipotle; the legal titles invoked were: *"Violation of California's False Advertising Act under California Business and Professional Code § 17500, and violation of California's Unfair Business Practice Act under California Business and Professional Code § 17200."*[21]

The abovementioned cases show how the conflict between vegetarian/vegan consumers and general sellers is actual and how it may lead to lawsuits, based on different laws in each country, while usually deriving from the principles of good faith, transparency, and correspondence between the products promoted and those actually delivered.

A Historic Victory

As an attorney, in 2015, I was contacted by a woman, a single parent, whose two-year-old son was expelled from a public nursery because she was a vegan and asked for a vegan option for her son. In order to obtain vegan food, the school required a medical certificate attesting the child's good health, and periodical analysis. None of those stipulations were placed on the other parents, and that, of course, represented a clear discrimination.

After the woman refused to make such certification, the school expelled her child, and I readily filed a claim at the Administrative Court (T.A.R.), stating that such a decision implied an unjustified discrimination, and a clear disproportion; our counterpart, the town of Merano, stated that such decision was intended to protect the child's health and that, therefore, such major interest would have prevailed over the mother's dietary choice.

My defense was based on the proof that a vegan diet is not only complete and proper for people of any age, but it is also better than the omnivorous, as it promotes good health and prevents many diseases, not to mention obesity.

Within a few days I obtained an interim order by the Court that obliged the school to re-enroll the child during the trial, while waiting for the final decision.

On July 24th, 2015, the Administrative Court of Bolzano upheld the claim, pronouncing the sentence no. 245/15 that declared unjust and undue the school's request and confirmed the child's re-enrollment.

Even if the Court did not enter into the health question, it is very important to observe that the town's argument was clearly discarded, given that, if the child's health had been in danger, the Court should have observed the *ubi maior, minor cessat* rule, recognizing as predominant the interest to life and health in place of ethics. That did not happen, and the town defense was not able to give any evidence of its statement that a vegan diet would have harmed the child.

The child is currently vegan, and he is attending the same nursery. This happy ending shows how a well-organized defense, deeply rooted in facts and scientific evidences, can overcome the prejudice in a courtroom.

The key for this success was, of course, the correct knowledge of the matter, as attorneys are usually scared to defend a vegan diet, since they are the first to condemn it, considering it inappropriate for children.

The American Dietetic Association publications were very useful in this case, as they represented a good scientific argument.

3.2 LEGAL PROTECTION
OF THE VEGETARIAN/VEGAN CONSUMER

Although there are many differences among legal systems, those of Western countries are very similar in many aspects. A comparison may be useful to understand the critical issues and to hypothesize future progress.

In Italy, for example, the legal relationship between customer and restaurateur represents a purchase, and it is disciplined by article no. 1470 of the Civil Code as the "*contract that has as its object the transfer of ownership of a thing or the transfer of rights in change of a price.*" This is both the purchase of food for immediate consumption (for example bar, restaurant, canteen, etc.), and the purchase as stock (supermarkets, vending machines, distance selling, etc.).

The warranty provided by article no. 1490 of the Civil Code states that: "*The seller is responsible for ensuring that the thing sold is free from defects that make it unsuitable for the use it is intended for, or that appreciably decrease the value.*" It is obviously similar to the American law invoked in the case *Gupta v. Asha Enterprises LLC* (specifically, NJSA 2A: 58C-1 to -11) and, in fact, about Italian warranty the conclusions are the same, namely that the non-vegetarian food sold as such is not unsuitable for the uses for which it is intended (eating), but simply that it lacks the requisites promised.

Therefore, if a vegetarian customer of a restaurant decides to sue the restaurateur, having received a dish containing meat (for example potato croquettes served with ham), even though he had made a request for vegetarian food, he could not act on the basis of article no. 1490 of the Civil Code. In this case the European Community Law will succor: the 99/44/EC directive currently governs the consumer reports, and its article no. 2 states the seller's obligations and warranties. The Italian Consumer Code (Legislative Decree 206/05, article no. 129), that makes applicable in Italy the European directive, states:

> The seller has the obligation to deliver the goods in conformity with the contract of sale. It is assumed that the goods are conform to the contract if, where relevant, the following circumstances exist:
>
> a) are fit for the purposes for which goods of the same type are normally used;
>
> b) comply with the description given by the seller and possess the qualities of goods which the seller has held out to the consumer as a sample or model;
>
> c) show the quality and performance which are normal in goods of the same type and which the consumer can reasonably expect, given the nature of the goods and, where appropriate, public statements on the specific characteristics of the goods made about them by the seller, the manufacturer, or its agent or representative, particularly in advertising or on labeling;
>
> d) are also suitable for the particular use that the consumer requires them and that he made known to the seller at the time of conclusion of the contract and that the seller has accepted, also implicitly.

§ b) and d) of article no. 129 Legislative Decree no. 206/05 contemplate exactly the case in question, namely that (b) the product does not meet the characteristics shown by the seller, or (d), even being in itself suitable for the purpose for which it is generally finalized (eating), it does not meet the needs of individual customers (eating for vegetarians).

The premise of the action in accordance with paragraph b) is that the seller may have suggested different quality from those actually possessed by the product. For example, the case does not occur if the customer buys a food believing that it is free from certain ingredients, based on their own self-belief.

Pursuant to paragraph d), even in the absence of a description making erroneous reliance, the consumer may sue the seller, in the case that the specific needs have been previously declared and that the seller, even knowing them, entered into the contract, also implicitly (for example by administering the food at the restaurant table).

Article no. 130 of Legislative Decree 206/05, which establishes the warranty rights of the consumer in the event of non-conformity of the product, provides two alternative remedies: repair/replacement or the termination of the contract, resulting in a refund of the price, just in case the first remedy is not possible or is too expensive.

In practice, therefore, both the customer at the restaurant and the buyer of packaged food have the right to request a replacement with another according to the wishes or promises, and if this is not possible, for example because such an alternative does not exist, he has the right to receive a refund.

As said above, this is a contractual relationship (buying and selling) and, therefore, any non-performance or improper performance of the seller determines the purchaser's right to compensation for damages suffered under article no. 1218 of the Civil Code:

> "A debtor who does not exactly fulfill the obligation due is obliged to reimburse damages, unless he can prove that the failure or delay was due to impossibility of performance resulting from causes beyond his control."

Like in the United States, criminal law may also be applied in Italy; in fact, article no. 515 of Penal Code (Fraudulent trading) states that:

> Whoever, in the course of a commercial activity, or in a shop open to the public, delivers a movable thing for another, or a movable, by origin, quality or quantity different from that stated or agreed, shall be punished, if the offense does not constitute a more serious offense, to imprisonment up to two years or to a fine up to € 2.065.

The Italian case law on the subject of fraudulent trading has come to interpretations rather extensive, so as to state that:

> The holding of frozen food in the refrigerator of a store and the omitted mention on the menu of this pre-condition of the food complements the attempted crime of fraudulent trading, given that the preparation of a list of food with no indication that some ingredients were frozen demonstrates the uniqueness and suitability of the action for the configuration of the offense in question. Moreover, since the activity of the keeper is aimed to offer to the public, to realize the attempt is not required any concrete relationship with the customer, because, in that case, would recur the hypothesis of the offense consumed. (Italian Penal Supreme Court Sect. III, March 2, 2004, no. 14806)

In addition, the Supreme Court stated that:

> On the subject of fraudulent trading, the term statement of art. 515 Penal Code also includes information about its origin, source, quality, or quantity of the goods contained in the eventual advertising message that preceded the offering for sale of the same material, so that advertisement is likely to mislead the buyer who receives the 'aliud pro alio.' (Court of Cassation pen. Sect. III Sent., 22 May, 2008, no. 27105)

Commercial fraud is apparent in every case in which the seller may have suggested to the buyer qualities that the product does not possess; receiving the false information that food does not contain meat, or that it is vegetarian or vegan, is included in such a case.

Comparing the McDonald's case with the Italian legal system, we can observe that in that case the article no. 515 of the Italian Penal Code should have been applicable, upon proof that the company had promoted the sale of a product by giving false prerogatives—of course, it would be possible to sanction alternatively the attempt itself (advertising) and the commission of the offense (purchase by one or more users).

Offenses consisting of misrepresentations and/or misleading representations of products sold are independent from any contractual relationship, being distinguished from civil rules stated on sales. Such conducts, as theoretically suitable to mislead and harm the public, are sanctioned even in the case that harmful consequences did not occur.

The European Community directives sanction liar commercial promotion, not just as a criminal offense, but also as civil and administrative infringements.

Article no. 2 b) of the Italian Legislative Decree no. 145/07 says:

> Implementation of Directive 2005/29/EC on unfair commercial practices between businesses and consumers in the internal market and amending Directives 84/450/EEC, 97/7/EC, 98/27/EC 2002/65/EC and Regulation (EC) n. 2006/2004," defines "Misleading advertising: any advertising which in any way, including its presentation, is likely to mislead the natural or legal persons to which is addressed or whom it reaches and which, because of its deceptive nature, is likely to affect their economic behavior or which, for this reason, it is likely to injure a competitor.

Article no. 3 states that, in order to determine whether advertising is misleading, the following should be considered:

> a) the characteristics of goods or services, such as their availability, nature, execution, composition, method, and date of manufacture or provision, fitness for purpose, uses, quantity, specification, geographical or commercial origin or the results that can be obtained with their use, or the results and material features of tests or checks carried out on the goods or services;
> b) the price or the manner in which it is calculated, and the conditions under which goods or services are provided;
> c) the category, attributes, and rights of the advertiser, such as his identity and assets, his qualifications, rights of intellectual and industrial property, all other rights over intangible assets related to the company or his awards and accolades.

It must therefore be concluded that the misleading nature of an advertisement may descend from several profiles, each of which will have to be assessed individually, and even if only one of the parameters considered are determined unreasonable, there will be an infringement.

In particular, point c) shows the relevance of circumstances not directly related with the good in itself, but which relate to different elements, such as deprivation, the quality of the operator, etc.

The Legislative Decree no. 145/07 is an instrument of protection for professionals, with respect to competitors who are engaged in unfair trade practices, while the Legislative Decree no. 206/05 provide protection for consumers against professionals.

Article no. 1 of Legislative Decree 146/07,

> Implementation of Directive 2005/29/EC on unfair commercial practices between businesses and consumers in the internal market and amending Directives 84/450/EEC, 97/7/EC, 98/27/EC 2002/65/EC and Regulation (EC) n. 2006/2004" which the amended Article no. 18 of the Legislative Decree 206/05, defines "materially distort the economic behavior of consumers: means using a commercial practice to appreciably impair the consumer's ability to make an informed decision, causing the consumer to take a transactional decision that would not have been taken otherwise.

The misconduct can manifest through actions or omissions (articles 21-22 of the Italian Consumer Code) are, for example, misleading actions discernible in the case of a product represented as vegetarian without being one, in that they are likely to set up *"a commercial practice that contains information that is untrue,"* having falsely represented the main characteristics of the product, such as its availability, benefits, risks, execution, composition, accessories, after-sale customer assistance, and the complaint handling, method, and date of manufacture or provision, delivery, fitness for purpose, uses, quantity, specification, geographical or commercial origin or the results to be expected from its use, or results and material features of tests or checks carried out on the product.

The different case of misleading omission occurs when the professional omits material information that the average consumer needs in this context, to take an informed transactional decision and causes or is likely to cause in this way the average consumer to take a transactional decision that he would not otherwise have taken, or even policies where these hides or provides in an unclear, unintelligible, ambiguous or untimely manner.

The unlawful conduct occurs in case of simultaneous existence of the abovementioned conducts and the eligibility to induce consumers into error, or at least to enter into a contract that otherwise would not have concluded. That case certainly occurs if a vegetarian consumer buys something and, (i) the seller has suggested the absence of animal products in that food and, (ii) the purchase is based on this information and would not have been concluded knowing the real characteristics of the product.

Apart from civil remedies of the contract termination and reimbursement of damages, and criminal remedies against incorrect traders, the law also provides administrative protection to consumers, administered by the Guarantor Authority for Competition and Market (AGCM).

The Guarantor, on the recommendation of an interested party, initiates an investigation to ascertain the merits of the claims and, if there is any breach inhibiting the spread of illicit promotional messages can be suspended, and the responsible condemned to fines from a minimum of € 5.000,00 and a maximum of € 500,000,00.

Which is the relationship between different forms of protection (civil, criminal and administrative)? Is it necessary to choose one, or can an action coexist with each other? In the first place, each action is based on a specific law, insomuch the basis will be different in each case.

Nothing prevents a vegetarian consumer from exercising the withdrawal (or resolution) and, at the same time, appeal to the authorities for possible criminal and administrative violations by the trader; the Court has, in fact, ruled that:

> The crime of fraud in exercise of business can compete with the administrative offenses provided by the legislation on misleading advertising in Legislative Decree no. 206 of 2005 (which replaced the previously existing Legislative Decree no. 74/1992) since the latter operates in a plane and responds to a "ratio" differ from those of the criminal offense, and it has a wider field of application of sanctions, because the sanction is provided regardless of the material delivery of "aliud pro alio," which is necessary for the existence of the crime. (Court of Cassation pen. Sect. III Sent., 22 May, 2008, n. 27105)

A typical example of misleading advertising on the subject of vegetarianism is the promotion of a certain food as vegetarian, while it is not, while a special case of injury (or, at least, assault) to the right to vegetarianism consists in misleading advertising of foodstuffs containing products of animal origin, to which are attributed characteristics such as "necessity," for example, by decantation of "unique" skills, alleged not to be found in other foods.

The abovementioned cases do not only diffuse the interests of all consumers, causing them to buy products that are deemed necessary, while they may even be harmful, but—if they involve food of animal origin—also contribute to spread in vegetarians (and omnivores) the conviction that vegetarianism is erroneous, however impractical and harmful to health.

In practice, the consumer, "forced" to feed on animal products by food advertising, can begin to feel the practice of vegetarianism is impossible or even abandon it; from a theoretical viewpoint, however, the effect is to contribute to the formation and persistence of negative persuasions about the vegetarian choice.

For the reasons frequently stated above, even associations in favor of vegetarianism take actions against unfair trade practices, such as in the case *League Anti Vivisection v. Mellin*, where the animal rights association LAV reported to Antitrust Authority the commercial made by the corporation of baby food, professing the need of the consumption of meat products by children.

The disputed promotional message stated: *"Due to its specific needs, your child needs iron of the flesh,"* showing newborn children taking Mellin homogenized meat.

LAV reported:

- misleading act pursuant to article no. 21 of Legislative Decree 206/05, paragraph 1, point b) and 4, consisting in the dissemination of information not corresponding to the truth, clearly intended to mislead the consumer about actual benefits of using the product;
- misleading omission pursuant to article no. 22 D. Decree 206/05, consisting in the omitted mention of alternatives to meat for iron intake and of the danger resulting from eating meat;
- danger for children pursuant to article no. 21, paragraph 4, Legislative Decree 206/05 which was identified in inducing the consumption of meat in newborns, resulting in addiction and introduction of a food injurious to health.
- In support of its claims, LAV produced and reported numerous medical and scientific claims to demonstrate that:
- iron supply for babies in a vegetarian diet is almost twice than that based on the consumption of Mellin homogenized meat;
- the iron in meat is not irreplaceable;
- because of the fungibility of iron from meat with vegetables, eating meat is not required;
- eating meat is harmful to the human body.

As a result of the above, *"the company Mellin suspended the campaign, pledging to take account of the comments for the next steps."*[22]

Similar initiatives have been undertaken against companies that advertise dairy products, stating that it is necessary and irreplaceable for humans.

LAV v. Mellin is only one of the newest cases. Many years ago, there was a similar situation, when the Italian Bovine Guaranteed Meat Consortium, in 1992, promoted eating meat as "indispensable." Surveillance authority agreed with the animal rights association, and advertisements were modified accordingly.

In 1997, the Plasmon company and the Italian Consortium of Slaughterers, respectively promoted chicken, turkey, lamb, and rabbit meat as baby suitable foods, defining them as "*an essential and irreplaceable food for the baby's growth, thanks to its high protein content and nutrition that is unmatched in other foods*" and beef as "*indispensable for its nutritional values.*" Both advertisements were changed after the intervention of the Institute of Advertising self-discipline.

At the conclusion of the above, the Consortium acknowledged the need "*to stop using the word 'essential' (or other similar words) to describe meat as food.*"

Apart from the vegetarians' right not to receive the imposition of a meal containing animal products, does its opposite exist, such as the right to not receive plant foods?

In 2004, Jamar L. Travillion, a prisoner at the Allegheny County Jail (USA), complained that he had received a vegetarian meal during the entire Lenten period, and that this would have forced him into a religious practice incompatible with his Protestant faith.

At the basis of the legal action undertaken by the prisoner toward the jail, *Travillion v. Allegheny County Bureau of Corrections et al.*, there was § 1983 of Civil Rights Act, which states:

> Every person who, under color or any statute, ordinance, regulation, custom or usage, of any State of Territory, subjects ... any citizen of the United States ... to the deprivation of any rights, privileges or immunities secured by the Constitution and laws, Shall be Liable to the party injured in an action at law, suit in equity, or other proper Proceeding for redress.

The negligent conduct by the penitentiary institution would have consisted in violation of the First Amendment of the US Bill of Rights, which guarantees freedom of worship.

The lawsuit, lost in the first degree, was then devolved to the judgment of the Court of Appeal, which finally ruled that: "*The eating of a vegetarian repast is not inherently linked to a religious practice. Regularly, Vegetarian meals are eaten by many different people on an everyday basis, regardless of their religion.*"[23]

The US courts have affirmed the principle according to which the vegetarian food does not distinguish any religion, being habitually consumed by people of any religion; there are, in short, religious or ethical positions that ban flesh, but not that would prohibit the consumption of plant foods.

The Court statement seems to affirm that there is no such thing as the "*right to non-vegetarianism,*" since no duty to abstain from eating vegetables is currently recognized under American laws.

3.3 A MANDATORY VEGETARIAN/VEGAN OPTION?

Premises

Eating involves both human rights and animal rights, and the latter could be protected by the prohibition of eating foods of animal origin, while vegetarians' rights can be protected providing an effective right to choose.

Excluding the possibility of providing a legal obligation to vegetarianism, many people ask for a law that allows vegetarians to pursue the vegetarian choice without restrictions or discrimination, thus promoting both the spread of this diet and the protection of those who practice it.

On the basis of the above, many animal advocacy associations have begun to campaign in favor of laws intended to protect the vegetarian/vegan choice as a right.

Given that it is impossible to imagine that any law could forbid the eating of meat, is it possible that a law could force any and all restaurateurs to make vegetarian/vegan option always available? This question was faced in Italy, in 2006, when the Italian association LAV (Anti-Vivisection League) promoted a bill for mandatory vegetarian/vegan option; this was one of the first cases, in the Western society, of a law made to try to protect vegetarian/vegan people and their choice.

In 2011 the Canadian animal advocacy association Animal Justice began to claim the recognition of such a choice in Ontario.

The abovementioned cases differ for many reasons, and represent different approaches to the same matter. A brief study and a comparison will be useful to determine if it is possible to obtain an actual law to guarantee a vegetarian/vegan option, and which would be the best way do that.

The Italian Bill on Vegetarian/Vegan Option

The bill was presented for the first time in the Italian Senate, in the XV Legislature, identified as DDL 1879, November 13, 2007, signed by Senator Valpiana.

The title chosen, *Rules for the protection of vegetarian and vegan food choices*, clearly shows the purpose and aims of the project, which takes into account both the regimes vegetarian and vegan.

The bill's preamble contains many insights drawn from the ethical, environmental, cultural, and health examined in the previous chapters, stating in part: *"Only in Italy, food consumption implies the death of more than 600 million animals from land and incalculable numbers of aquatic animals (fish, molluscs, crustaceans). Factory farms are also a major source of pollution of groundwater and of the atmosphere."*[24]

In addition to the instances for animals, there are also environmental and social issues statements: *"The vegetarian or vegan lifestyle also helps to promote a more equitable distribution of resources that could help fight world hunger. Much of cereal production in the Southern Hemisphere, in fact, are intended to feed animals for meat production in Western countries, when they could cover local needs."*[25]

A broader discussion includes health issues related to diet.

> Science, both official and independent, recognizes to a healthy, well-balanced vegetarian and vegan diet the capacity to ensure a better state of health than the diet that includes meat (eighty pounds a year per capita) or fish (more than twenty pounds per year). It is shown that a vegetarian diet, rich in fruits and vegetables, protects against cardiovascular disease by 24 percent and decreases the chances of heart attack, one of the leading causes of death in Western countries, favored by a diet too rich in fats and animal proteins. The incidence of the most prevalent cancers (colorectal, breast, prostate, pancreas) is much higher among people who eat animal foods (70 percent of people affected by these diseases) rather than among vegetarians (only 30 percent). The Western vegetarians also have a lower incidence of obesity and diabetes in comparison to omnivores.[26]

The need of providing a legislative protection in terms of vegetarianism, however, is not based solely on ethical consideration or health benefits, but also on the instances of a relevant part of the population, stating that:

> In Italy the number of vegetarians and vegans is rapidly increasing: in recent years, since 2002, have doubled, rising from three million to six million.
> Failing to find complete and balanced meals without meat, fish, or ingredients of animal origin are forced to frugal meals and nutritionally unbalanced in contradiction with the principles of equality enshrined in the Constitution, according to which the state and the government must ensure the same treatment to all citizens, regardless of gender, religion, and every other kind of guidance. Ensuring alternative vegetarian food.

On the abovesaid premises, the bill's core is as follows:

Article 1 (Purposes)

1. This law protects vegetarian and vegan diet and Citizens who follow them and affirms and promotes ethical and scientific aspects of such choices.

Article 2 (Definitions)

1. For the purposes of this Act is defined:

a. vegetarian, diet that excludes meat, fish, and other foods derived from the killing of animals;
b. vegan, diet that excludes meat, fish, and other foods derived from the killing of animals, milk and dairy products, eggs, honey, and other foods of animal origin.

Article 3 (Refectories)

1. In all public refectories, affiliated and private, or exercising any kind of public service, refectories performing service for schools of all levels, including nurseries, universities, refectories, and places where workers are forced to eat, being unable to return for lunch at home, such as bars and restaurants conventioned with workplaces, will always be offered and advertised at least one vegetarian option and a vegan alternative to foods or products containing animal ingredients provided in the conventional menu.
2. The vegetarian and vegan menu offered must be structured in such a way as to ensure a balanced intake of all nutrients as indicated by official science of nutrition and considering scientific advances in this field.
3. The vegetarian and vegan food should not even contain ingredients of animal origin used in the preparation and unidentifiable organoleptically, listed in the Annex.
4. In order to ensure an adequate service to users, the staff responsible for the administration is adequately informed of the purposes of this law.
5. The eggs present in vegetarian food must come from hens organically raised or outdoors.

Article 4.

(Education and schooling)

1. Within the school year following the year in progress at the date of issue of this Act, the Ministry of Education, University, and Research places the teaching of fundamentals of nutrition, food, and vegetarian and vegan food in the teaching programs for vocational institutes and vocational institutes for hotel services and catering.
2. Students who, in obedience to conscience, in the exercise of the right to freedom of thought, conscience and religion, recognized by the Universal Declaration of Human rights, the Convention for the Protection of Human rights and Fundamental Freedoms and the International Covenant relating to civil and political rights, are opposed to violence

against all living beings, can declare their conscientious objection to lessons teaching practices regarding food animals.
3. The institutions indicated in paragraph 1 shall be obliged to make known to all students their right to exercise conscientious objection referred to in paragraph 2.
4. No student objector may suffer adverse consequences due to the exercise of the right indicated in paragraph 2.
5. Students objectors are offered a proposal to integrate alternative study the number of hours required by the school curriculum.

Currently, the bill is pending upon the Parliament, and real prospects of approval are unknown, while it does not seem to have been at the center of special attention by the Parliament, also considering the many conflicting interests, starting from the food industry.

Of course, the food industry, in particular that of meat and meat products, is strong enough in an economic and political sense to represent a significant obstacle to any initiative, and it is also for this reason that, at present, the approval of the bill seems improbable.

On the other hand, the benefit from and the potential for economic growth and virtuosity inherent in the vegetarian culture, even in the legislative field, could be the best tool of the reasons underlying the bill.

The Canadian Reform

The Italian approach to the vegetarian/vegan option is based on the fact that the Italian Constitution already guarantees and promotes ethical, as well as religious, instances.

In Ontario the Human Rights Code, Part I, article 1, states as follows:

> Every person has a right to equal treatment with respect to services, goods and facilities, without discrimination because of race, ancestry, place of origin, colour, ethnic origin, citizenship, creed, sex, sexual orientation, gender identity, gender expression, age, marital status, family status, or disability. [27]

When Animal Justice, in 2011, began to claim the recognition of vegetarianism/veganism as a human right, the instance was connected with the abovementioned provision, and, particularly, around the interpretation of the word "creed."[28]

It is clear that the original provision was general, and that interpretation, therefore, played a key role to translate the general principle into actual rules and/or decisions.

The basic interpretation of the term "creed" was obviously connected with religion, but it is evident that, in this way, only the instances made by those who choose vegetarianism for religious reasons may be allowed.

The Ontario Human Rights Commission is the institution that, compiling the *Policy on preventing discrimination based on creed*, makes the actual human rights principles: as the same Commission states, "*The Code does not define creed, but the courts and tribunals have often referred to religious beliefs and practices.*"[29] In other words, although the term "creed" is not defined by the law, its actual meaning is based on the jurisprudential interpretation, and, until the last reform, it was strictly connected with religious beliefs.

In September 2015, the Commission finally approved ethical instances, and therefore introduced a new statement in its policy: "*Creed may also include non-religious belief systems that, like religion, substantially influence a person's identity, worldview, and way of life.*"[30]

The Commission policy is intended to guide the conduct of those who are offering services to the people, so that nobody could be discriminated against.

Some consider the Canadian reform as a victory (the first?) for the affirmation of the legal right to vegetarianism/veganism. Should we agree? First, we need to note that this is not a binding rule: it is only the Human Rights Tribunal of Ontario, which decide human rights claims.

Considering its non-binding nature, and the fact that it is not final (as the Tribunal may disregard it), the new policy is, of course, good news, but it does not represent a revolution at all.

It appears that the lack of any concern, in the Human Rights Code, for ethical rights, alongside those religious, represented a serious gap and a discrimination between religious and non-religious people; although the change was promoted by an animal advocacy association, and aimed to guarantee the right to vegan options, the consequences are not limited to such cases.

The fact that the Italian constitution provided a full recognition of ethics, as well as religion, from the beginning, explains why the two reforms are so different; while the first is a deep specification of actual duties, the second is still general and of principle.

Once the principle of non-discrimination against vegetarian/vegan people is affirmed, the question becomes: "*How are those people discriminated against?*"

The bottom line is that, as well as we recognize human rights, we cannot deny that such rights must include vegetarianism/veganism, intended as a profound moral instance; taking this for granted, the legislator has to define more specific rules to prevent any discrimination, as it happened for discrimination based on race, gender, etc.

One of the main issues practically encountered regards the definition of "equivalent," that is the core problem with discrimination; in fact, once that we found our vegan option, the problem is whether or not it looks/nourishes as well as its animal counterpart.

3.4 DIETARY GUIDELINES

Many obstacles to the complete eradication of any discrimination derive from nutritional concerns that lead one to conclude that a vegetarian, or (particularly) a vegan diet, is unbalanced and unhealthy.

Some countries adopted a system of dietary guidelines, to educate citizens, and particularly children, to the correct dietary habits.

Although the guidelines are not binding, if followed properly, they may represent a good reference in the most controversial cases, and, above all, the specification of the abovesaid principles included the right to health.

One of the main reasons of such documents is the concern about the growing phenomenon of childhood obesity, typical of the Western societies, and largely caused by the spread of erroneous models and high-calorie foods, especially compared to the modern low physical activity.

Italian guidelines show to embrace the abovesaid concern:

> The Guidelines for the national school food move from the need to facilitate, since childhood, adoption of healthy eating habits for health promotion and prevention of chronic degenerative diseases (diabetes, cardiovascular disease, obesity, osteoporosis, etc.) caused by bad nutrition. On the other hand, the profound changes in lifestyle of families and individuals have led to an increasing number of individuals with the need to consume at least one meal away from home, using the services of catering and commercial. [31]

Scientists from all around the world, especially in the West, are trying to understand the relationship between meat consumption and the obesity rate of the population. The study published in June 2009 in England by the National Institutes of Health has identified the consumption of meat as the cause of approximately 30% higher risk to develop obesity. [32]

Childhood is particularly sensitive with regard to food issues, both for the natural exposure of children to specific disorders or diseases, both for root habits which, if incorrect, may accompany the individual for most or the whole of his life.

From a nutritional point, the ministerial document was completely omitted to consider the issue of vegetarianism, focusing rather on the properties of individual foods and, in particular, on the contribution of nutrients.

Even if vegetarianism is not specifically mentioned, the guidelines contain a generic reference to *"ethical-religious"* needs, where the vegetarian/ vegan choice is undoubtedly included and, therefore, recognized and protected like any other:

The standard of the service, the right of access for users with special health care needs and ethical-religious, must be maintained and defined in each business model, and declared to all users, to official control, to canteen committees, through a service charter" and "The operating model required to be identified in relation to the population is facing, defining the numerical size of the users, ages, physiological needs, pathological, ethical religious, any disability.[33]

The protected interest is, of course, respect of the opinions and of health; in this respect the scope of the reference appears to be deliberately broad and undefined, so potentially unlimited coverage.

What appears to be of undoubted importance is the obligation of providing information to all users; often the exercise of a right, especially if it is not well known or easily knowable, depends on the awareness of the owner, as it is evident that no one can exercise a right of which the existence is ignored.

On purely legal grounds, it may be asked if such provisions can establish a genuine right, or simply an option. It seems that they represent the mere transposition of fundamental constitutional principles and, as such, cannot be considered real sources in establishing those rights, rather representing a technical and systematic discipline.

It can therefore be argued that the vegetarian-vegan choice should be implemented in the school feeding program, of course, as well as religious instances to abstain from certain foods, but also—at least theoretically—to those ethics even more restrictive, for example fruitarianism.

Consistent with the above, the document also states that: *"They also assured adequate food substitutions related to ethical and religious or cultural reasons. These replacements do not require medical certification, but the simple request of the parents."*[34]

In the latter reference the mention of health needs disappears, and cultural instances are mentioned for the first time; the word seems correct and appropriate, given that many eating habits depend not only on ethical or religious beliefs, but also by cultural substratum.

The scope of the provision is broad and unambiguous. Refectories are required to ensure the presence of an *"adequate replacement,"* which will have the nutritional adequacy and therefore qualitative-quantitative similar to "normal" dishes.

Since the criteria to be observed in nutritional composition of meals are provided and described in the guidelines, it seems clear that the assessment of adequacy is to be made on the basis of these parameters, allowing each user to enjoy the same number of courses and a similar nutritional intake.

Considering vegetarian/vegan alternatives, it should be emphasized that the proper replacement should also include all the variety of foods, and this is not only to allow the proper intake and the necessary diversification, but also for social and psychological issues. The significance of these issues cannot be neglected, especially in the school context, where users are youths, exposed to continuous confrontation with their classmates.

Moreover, the vegetarian/vegan option (even considering just human perspective) should not be considered just as a matter of respect for the opinions and choices of the users, but, supremely, for health benefits and ecological implications, which are also referred to repeatedly in the document.

It seems contradictory that even the management of waste is inspired to ecological criteria, while nothing is said about the environmental impact of food derived from animals.

Finally, the omission of any reference to the health aspects of vegetarianism seems unreasonable, both in terms of nutrition education, and for its many benefits in the growth phase and into adulthood. In this regard, it should be noted that the erroneous conviction of the danger of a vegetarian diet by children often prevails in school environments; that determines a prejudice resulting in a sort of mere "tolerance," sometimes with ill-concealed concern for the (alleged) health problems of the children.

The American Dietary Guidelines

A comparison between Italian and US Dietary Guidelines may be useful. In 2010 the US Department of Health and Human Services published the *Dietary Guidelines*, which are described as follows: *"The Dietary Guidelines for Americans, 2010, provides evidence-based nutrition information and advice for people age 2 and older. They serve as the basis for Federal food and nutrition education programs."*[35]

In contrast with the Italian model, there is no reference to cultural, environmental, or social, while the question related to health is emphasized. That seems consistent with the different style of eating, inextricably linked to fast food, which, in turn, is more often connected to junk food.

The American document, even apart from any environmental or ethical considerations, unlike the Italian, gives more consideration to vegetarianism, starting from the scientific aspects:

> *In prospective studies of adults, compared to non-vegetarian eating patterns, vegetarian-style eating patterns have been associated with improved health outcomes—lower levels of obesity, a reduced risk of cardiovascular disease, and lower total mortality. Several clinical trials have documented that vegetarian eating patterns lower blood pressure."*[36]

On the basis of the above, the US guidelines say, therefore, that:

> The USDA Food Patterns allow for additional flexibility in choices through their adaptations for vegetarians—a vegan pattern that contains only plant foods and a lacto-ovo vegetarian pattern that includes milk and milk products

and eggs. The adaptions include changes in the protein foods group and, in the vegan adaptation, in the dairy group. The changes made in the protein foods group at the 2,000 calorie level are shown in Table 5-3. The vegan dairy group includes calcium-fortified beverages and foods commonly used as substitutes for milk and milk products. Complete patterns at all calorie levels are shown in Appendices 8 and 9. These vegetarian variations represent healthy eating patterns, but rely on fortified foods for some nutrients. In the vegan patterns especially, fortified foods provide much of the calcium and vitamin B12, and either fortified foods or supplements should be selected to provide adequate intake of these nutrients.[37]

What developments would be desirable for ministerial guidelines? First, as mentioned above, to enhance and emphasize all aspects of ethical and ecological already treated.

The vegetarian alternative, and, even more, the vegan, combine issues related to culture, religious, ethical, medical, environmental, and health benefits; the majority of foreclosures food of a religious (Hinduism, Judaism, Islam, etc.), in fact, covers meat or, more in general, animals.

What position might ministerial guidelines find, in case of an issue of the bill? Since it is a guidance document, it does not contradict with the enactment of framework legislation, and therefore could well maintain its function and, indeed, rise to the subject of referral legislation for specifics technical in nature.

In short, if the bill enters into force, it would be possible to coordinate it with documents of a technical-scientific and administrative, such as to facilitate its application and to contain all the specific upgrades and enhancements of the case.

In light of the above, it would even be desirable to amend the bill to make a referral to the ministerial decrees, which are definitely more versatile and effective in practice and could benefit from the innovations in science and food products, continually developing enough thought of the increasing market penetration of alternative foods for vegetarians and the consequent opportunity to change, to renew and extend the offer of menus free of animal foods.

NOTES

1. *Corriere della Sera*, 8/10/99, p. 17.
2. Ibid., 9/10/99, p. 14.
3. Ibid., 9/10/99, p. 14.
4. *La Stampa*, 9/10/99, p. 12.
5. *Corriere della sera*, 9/10/99, p. 14.
6. http://www.repubblica.it/cronaca/2011/04/29/news/inchiesta_italiana-15507476/
7. http://www.thisislondon.co.uk/standard/article-23825755-social-workers-said-no-meat-no-dairy-diet-was-starving-our-three-year-old-son.do

8. http://www.news.com.au/lifestyle/real-life/vegetarian-couple-barred-from-adopting-in-greece/story-e6frflri-1226019462255

9. http://firenze.repubblica.it/cronaca/2012/01/12/news/il_tribunale_tedesco_affida_bimba_a_pap_la_mamma_si_barrica_in_casa_con_la_bimba-28013026/

10. http://iltirreno.gelocal.it/regione/2012/01/31/news/una-legge-nazista-vuole-prendere-la-mia-jasmin-1.3127700

11. Schlosser, *Fast Food Nation*, Houghton Mifflin, 2001, p. 123.

12. http://www.compassionatespirit.com/McDonalds-Lawsuit-article.htm

13. http://animalrights.about.com/b/2011/10/26/mcdonalds-french-fries-still-not-vegetarian.htm.

14. http://www.edcombs.com/CM/Notices/Notices150.asp

15. http://www.edcombs.com/CM/Notices/Notices166.asp

16. http://www.edcombs.com/CM/Notices/Notices168.asp

17. http://lawyersusaonline.com/benchmarks/2011/07/

18. http://www.leagle.com/xmlResult.aspx?page=2& xmldoc=In%20NJCO%2020110718207.xml&docbase=CsLwAr3-2007-Curr&SizeDisp=7

19. http://lawmrh.wordpress.com/2011/09/26/another-food-suit-this-time-its-frijoles-rice-and-coconut-water/

20. http://docs.justia.com/cases/federal/districtourts/california/cacdce/2:2010cv02367/468825/20/0.pdf?1276236775

21. http://docs.justia.com/cases/federal/districtcourts/california/cacdce/2:2011cv07835/512689/8/0.pdf?1317455154. § 17500 of California Business and Professional Code states: "*It is unlawful for any person, firm, corporation or association, or any employee thereof with intent directly or indirectly to dispose of real or personal property or to perform services, professional or otherwise, or anything of any nature whatsoever or to induce the public to enter into any obligation relating thereto, to make or disseminate or cause to be made or disseminated before the public in this state, or to make or disseminate or cause to be made or disseminated from this state before the public in any state, in any newspaper or other publication, or any advertising device, or by public outcry or proclamation, or in any other manner or means whatever, including over the Internet, any statement, concerning that real or personal property or those services, professional or otherwise, or concerning any circumstance or matter of fact connected with the proposed performance or disposition thereof, which is untrue or misleading, and which is known, or which by the exercise of reasonable care should be known, to be untrue or misleading, or for any person, firm, or corporation to so make or disseminate or cause to be so made or disseminated any such statement as part of a plan or scheme with the intent not to sell that personal property or those services, professional or otherwise, so advertised at the price stated therein, or as so advertised. Any violation of the provisions of this section is a misdemeanor punishable by imprisonment in the county jail not exceeding six months, or by a fine not exceeding two thousand five hundred dollars ($2,500), or by both that imprisonment and fine.*"

22. http://www.primaonline.it/2011/12/13/99072/lav-carne-non-indispensabile-per-bambini-mellin-sospende-lo-spot-tv/

23. http://www.ca3.uscourts.gov/opinarch/062136np.pdf

24. About the unsustainability of eating meat/animal products: Hoogenkamp, Henk W., *Soy protein and formulated meat products*, CABI, Cambridge, USA, 2005, and Hui, Y. H., Nip, W.K., Rogers, R. W., Meat Science and Applications, Marcel Dekker, NY, USA, 2005. See also FAO, Livestock's Long Shadow, 2006, ftp://ftp.fao.org/docrep/fao/010/a0701e/a0701e00.pdf, World Watch Institute, *State of the World 2009*, Earthscan, UK, 2009. See also: Myers, Norman, *The hamburger connection: how Central America's forests became North America's hamburgers,* in *Ambio*, vol. 10, n. 1, 1981, Royal Swedish Academy of Sciences, p. 2-8, and Kaimowitz, Mertens, Wunder, Pacheco, *Hamburger Connection Fuels Amazon Destruction*, CIFOR, Center for International Forestry Research, aprile 2003 http://www.cifor.org/publications/pdf_files/media/Amazon.pdf.

25. Moore Lappé, *Diet For a Small Planet*, Ballantine Books, New York, USA, 1982, pp.69-71. See also: Burley, Helen, *What Feeds Our Food?*, Friends of the Earth, London, UK, 2008, p. 17.

26. See American Dietetic Association 2009 statements about vegetarianism and veganism and health http://www.vrg.org/nutrition/2009_ADA_position_paper.pdf.

27. https://www.ontario.ca/laws/statute/90h19

28. http://www.huffingtonpost.ca/camille-labchuk/veganism-ontario-human-right_b_8950052.html

29. http://www.ohrc.on.ca/en/policy-preventing-discrimination-based-creed

30. Ibid.

31. *National Nutritional Guidelines*, p. 5.

32. http://www.ncbi.nlm.nih.gov/pmc/articles/PMC2697260/?tool=pubmed

33. Ibid., p. 20.

34. Ibid., p. 22.

35. http://health.gov/dietaryguidelines/

36. *Dietary Guidelines*, p. 45.

37. Ibid., p. 53.

Conclusions

This work was intended to provide answers to certain questions, examining animal rights and vegetarianism/veganism mainly in their philosophical and legal implications.

The first consideration that emerges is that the philosophical doctrines of animal rights have no reflections in any Western legal system, which, however, accept a welfarist model, placing the human being at the center of protected interests, and only incidentally, the animals as nonhuman objects.

To date, in the light of history, it seems that the solution proposed by Francione is the most correct in terms of logic: only the abolition of the legal status of property can allow the realization in the regulatory framework of a real discipline of animal rights.

Analyzing the main philosophies about relations between human and nonhuman animals, it seems that much has been said and that, especially from the scientific revolution, the debate has been enriched with new arguments (both for and against) and instruments.

It appears obvious that, in a human society, the term "right" indicates an artificial construction by human beings and that, therefore, correlated to it, purely and simply, represents an artificial right to other animals; in this sense Bobbio's statement that animal rights are based on the will of the society, rather than on assumptions of nature is correct.

On the other hand, the question of animal rights could be inverted and, using the same arguments as above, could be considered at an impasse— which might be the foundation of the human right to dispose of nonhumans?

Denying the natural origin of the right, instead anchoring it in the consent of the associates, if it is not true that a human cannot attend these rights, the converse is also true: any act of disposal from humans to nonhumans cannot be placed in the conceptual category of the right, being arbitrary.

The proof of the above is that, even in investigating the moral and philosophical issues underlying the human-nonhuman interactions, there is not a single way of thinking, but the varied ones considered here (and, indeed, many more).

What major thinkers do agree on, regarding animal rights, is certainly that their right to life matches our duty to abstain from using them for food purposes.

In the above logic, vegetarianism, with all its implications, is fundamental and becomes the real philosophical pillar, being comparable, by relevance, with the prohibition to kill individuals of the same species, which is contained in all human societies.

If vegetarianism is, first, the recognition of the right of nonhumans to exist, veganism also implies respect for the right not to suffer, to freedom, and not to be treated as things, as well as the same right to life; at this point, it should be clear that any and all animals used for food purposes, even dairy and eggs, are part of the same chain of death.

Veganism as a moral duty exists within the philosophical currents of animal rights, but it is not yet expressly recognized by any law, since all animals are still considered properties.

Vegetarianism/veganism, from the point of view of the humans who embrace it, is a right, though the issue is far from devoid of controversy.

First, we tried to understand whether such a right, as Bobbio argued, represents the mere assertion of an expectation, waiting to be recognized by positive, or if it may be considered a real existing legal institution.

At present there are no laws about the so-called "right to vegetarianism." Does this mean that the vegetarian does not have any legal foothold to establish their case?

The conclusion of this work is that the legal means necessary and sufficient to recognize the right of each to claim food not of animal origin lies on human rights, currently recognized in the Western countries.

What positive law seems to lack is undoubtedly the specification and the exact identification of pipelines, requirements, and obligations necessary to translate the abovesaid principles in everyday life.

In a complex society such as we have today, it is increasingly common that the enunciation of a freedom not match the real possibilities of concrete exercise, and this is probably the case of vegetarianism, since, in the absence of vegetable alternatives to the foods of animal origin, the freedom of the individual is limited or even prohibited.

Recognizing vegetarianism as a right rather than as a mere freedom would imply that the Legislature effected by means of adequate standards to permit the effective enjoyment, rather than simply not creating obstacles.

The second question is whether vegetarianism is legally relevant and which claims vegetarians can affirm with respect to other associates and, in particular, to economic operators that produce, sell, and provide food.

Would a mandatory vegetarian/vegan option be applicable today? Regan, in this regard, said: *"In a capitalist economy, in the current circumstances, I do not see how it is possible to force restaurant owners to offer options for vegetarians or vegans. To people who require the option of a vegetable dish, the free market responds: 'Eat where you'll find.'"*

Regan's statement is clear and, from a point of view, true, but between an autonomous and a heteronomous fulfillment (imposed by law), there are many differences that cannot be silenced.

First, the spontaneous adoption by operators of plant foods as alternative to those of animal origin could not concern the whole market, and, therefore, that would not abolish the discrimination; there would be an increase of places of possible purchase/consumption of food, but for a vegetarian, it would not be possible to go anywhere or make use of any service without a prior check.

The greatest difficulties arising from the legal vacuum in this area, which could not be exceeded in the case of spontaneous market adjustment, covers all cases in which the user is forced to buy or have a meal in a certain place, or in a structure—in many cases there are not alternatives, such as schools, military, hospitals, and catering service businesses.

Once established that a right to vegetarianism already exists, at least where the most important human rights are granted, it can be said that a specific codification would be, at least, very useful. Even if there is no reason to doubt that the vegetarian/vegan consumer has the right to claim the exercise of such choice, only the elimination of any discrimination would allow one to fully exercise such a right.

The food discrimination against those who make a vegetarian/vegan choice does not only consist in the lack of alternatives, but also in alternatives unsuitable or different in form and/or substance, so as to make the choice extremely limiting.

What are the prospects of a law about vegetarian/vegan options? If, as it seems, the number of vegetarians is increasing and the market of "alternative" food is also, it is legitimate to assume that the support will grow, while the opposition will decrease.

In terms of legislative policy, it does not seem that there are particular obstacles to the introduction of an alternative that would not restrict the choice of who is omnivorous, rather expanding it.

Economic issues are likely to be those most affected by the implementation of the rules on vegetarianism, and, probably, the major manufacturers/distributors would see this as a threat of their own market position.

The provision of a legal obligation to provide a structured plant food would be likely to open the door to new markets, or at least to promote the acceptance and expansion of what are now products and niche manufacturers.

The US Department of Agriculture (USDA) supports zootechnics at various stages:

> "Milk producers benefit from their own set of federal subsidy programs. Subsidies in various forms to dairy producers totaled $4.8 billion between 1995 and 2009. This included emergency supplemental "market loss" payments of $1 billion to compensate dairy producers for low prices between 1999 and 2001. In 2002, Congress enacted the Milk Income Loss Contract (MILC) program to make these supports permanent, which provides direct payments for dairy producers when the average monthly price of milk falls below a set level.
>
> "In addition, through the Dairy Product Price Support Program, the USDA protects producers from price declines by purchasing surplus products from dairy processors. The federal government also artificially controls the price of milk through milk marketing orders, which set minimum prices that processors who sell milk must pay in specified areas, depending on the intended use of the milk."[1]

Farmers receive much support: the Livestock Compensation Program, the Emergency Livestock Feed Assistance, and the Livestock Emergency Assistance Program. Between 1995 and 2009 farmers received about $3.5 billion in funding.[2]

A full right to vegetarianism implies that not even the tax dollars from ethical contributors could finance the meat industry, and governs adopting a non-discriminatory system of supports, avoiding distorting the market.

We can also say that laws about ethical options will increase the competition in the food sector, encouraging lower prices and a variety of offers.

Apart from the fact that vegetarianism is considered an actual right and that, therefore, an active legal protection is provided, it would be sufficient to recognize it as a mere freedom to conclude that the current regulatory system, especially in taxation, encouraging the production of animal foods in place of those plants, is an obstacle to the effective exercise of this freedom.

Encouraging those who produce or choose to eat animal products determines the corresponding discrimination of vegetarians, making it even more costly economically, and thus limiting the exercise of an incompressible freedom of choice.

While the law faces one of the main issues of animal rights, there are already new perspectives and implications, such as the production of *in-vitro meat*.

If this kind of production—already the subject of several patents—is accepted, maybe there will be a new category of consumers, known as "vitro-vegetarian," to take into account by the law.

NOTES

1. http://www.pcrm.org/health/reports/agriculture-and-health-policies-unhealthful-foods
2. Ibid.

Bibliography

Allen Fox, Michael, *Deep Vegetarianism*, Temple University Press, Philadelphia, 1999.
Antolisei, Francesco, *Manuale di diritto penale*, quindicesima edizione, parte generale, Giuffrè, Milano, 2003.
Antolisei, Francesco, *Manuale di diritto penale*, quindicesima edizione, parte speciale, Giuffrè, Milano, 2003.
Asimov, I., Silverberg, R., *Robot NDR-113*, Bompiani, Milano, 1992.
Attali, Jacques, Lessico per il futuro, Armando Editore, Roma, 1999.
Baker, Joanne, *50 Grandi idee Universo*, trad. A. Migliori, Dedalo, Bari, 2011.
Baldwin, Cheryl J., *Sustainability in the Food Industry*, IFT Press, Washington, 2009.
Barberis, Mauro, *Breve storia della filosofia del diritto*, Il Mulino, Bologna, 2004.
Battaglia, Luisella, *Etica e diritti degli animali*, Laterza, Bari, 1997.
Bekoff, Marc, Pierce, Jessica, *Giustizia Selvaggia – La vita morale degli animali*, B. C. Dalai Editore, Milano, 2010.
Bentham, Jeremy, *An Introduction to the Principles of Morals and Legislation* [1780] , Dover, New York, 2007.
Bhikhu C. Parekh, *Jeremy Bentham, Critical Assessments*, Routledge, 1993.
Block, Sharma, Aingh et al vs. McDonald's, Edelman, Combs, Latturner & Goodwin, LLC., www.edcombs.com/CM/Notices/Notices150.asp (last consultation on 12/10/2012).
Bobbio, Norberto, *Da destra e sinistra*, Donzelli, Roma, 1994.
B obbio, Norberto, *Diritti dell'uomo e società* , in "Sociologia del diritto", 1989, n. 1, pag. 25.
Bobbio, Norberto, *L'età dei diritti*, Einaudi, Torino, 1990.
Bonnot de Condillac, Etienne, *Traitè des animaux*, 1755.
Bordon, Raniero, Rossi, Stefano, Tramontano, Luigi, *La nuova responsabilità civile. Casualità. Responsabilità oggettiva. Lavoro*, UTET Giuridica, Torino, 2002.
Bortoluzzi, Daniela, *Impronte di Gesù*, Eremon Edizioni, Latina, 2008.
Burley, Helen, *What feeds our food?*, Friends of the Earth, London, 2008.
Cadoppi, Alberto, a cura di, *Trattato di diritto penale - Parte speciale Vol. VI: Delitti contro la moralità pubblica, di prostituzione, contro il sentimento per gli animali e contro la famiglia*, UTET Giuridica, Torino, 2010.
Campbell, T. Colin, Campbell, Thomas M., *The China Study*, BenBella Books, Dallas, 2006.
Canciani, Mario, *Ultima cena dagli Esseni: una documentata nuova esplorazione*, Edizioni Mediterranee, Roma, 1995.
Cardinale Giuseppe Agostino Orsi, *Storia Ecclesiastica*, Giuseppe Battaggia, Venezia, 1826.
Cartesio, *Meditazioni Metafisiche*, Ed. Armando, Roma, 2008.
Catarci, Scarpato, Simeone, *Sostenibilità ambientale ed economica nel mercato del tonno rosso*, Franco Angeli Editore, Milano, 2007.

Cendon, Paolo, *Il risarcimento del danno non patrimoniale, parte speciale*, UTET Giuridica, Torino, 2009.

Charles, Jay Daryl, *The Unformed Conscience of Evangelism: Recovering the Church's Moral Vision*, Intervarsity Press, 2002.

Civitello, Linda, *Cuisine and Culture: a History of Food and People*, John Wiley and Sons, Hoboken, 2008.

Cocchi, Antonio, *Del vitto pitagorico per uso della medicina*, Simone Occhi, Venezia, 1743.

Comunicazione della Commissione al Consiglio e al Parlamento Europeo: Una strategia per lo sviluppo sostenibile dell'acquacultura europea, Bruxelles, 2002.

Cuffaro, Vincenzo, *Responsabilità civile*, IPSOA, Milano, 2007.

Cummings, Louise, *Rethinking the BSE crisis*, London, Springer, 2010.

Davies, Paul, *Una fortuna cosmica. La vita nell'universo: coincidenza o progetto divino?*, Mondadori, Milano, 2007.

De Matteis, G., *La strage silenziosa dei delfini con le reti a strascico*, La Repubblica, ricerca.repubblica.it/repubblica/archivio/repubblica/2011/07/30/la-strage-silenziosa-dei-delfini-reti-strascico.html (last consultation on 12/10/2012)

De Rachewiltz, Boris, *Il libro dei morti degli antichi egizi*, Edizioni Mediterranee, Roma, 1992.

De Waal, Franz, *Good Natured: The Origins of Right and Wrong in Humans and Other Animals*, Harvard University Press, 1997.

Derrickson, Scott, *The Day the Earth Stood Still*, lungometraggio, Twentieth Century Fox, 2008.

Descartes, *Discourse on the Method*, SMK Books, 2009.

Desjardins, Joseph R., *Environmental ethics*, Boston, 2001.

Elisabetta Basile, Claudio Cecchi, *Diritto all'alimentazione agricoltura e sviluppo*, Franco Angeli Editore, Milano, 2006.

Erasmo, *Dulce bellum inexpertis*, in *Adagiorum Chiliades tres*, Venezia, Manuzio, 1508, trad. it. Di S. Seidel Menchi col titolo *Chi ama la guerra non l'ha vista in faccia*, in *Adagia*, Torino, Einaudi, 1980.

Escherichia Coli O157:H7 e altri ceppi verocitotossici, Sicurezza degli alimenti, www.sicurezzadegl ialimenti. it/ ecoliO157H7.htm (last consultation on 12/10/2012)

Fairlie, Simon, *Meat: a Benign Extravagance*, Chelsea Green Publishing Company, White River Junction, 2010.

Fanciotti, Marco, *La Chiesa e gli animali*, Gruppo Perdisa Editore, Bologna, 2007.

Fenchel, Tom, *The Origin and Early Evolution of Life*, Oxford University Press, 2003.

Ferrajoli, Luigi a cura di E. Vitale, *Diritti fondamentali. Un dibattito teorico*, Roma-Bari, Laterza, I ed., 2001.

Ferrajoli, Luigi, *Dai diritti del cittadino ai diritti della persona*, in Zolo, D. (a cura di), *La cittadinanza. Appartenenza, identità, diritti*, Roma-Bari, Laterza, 1999.

Ferrero, L., *Storia del Pitagorismo nel mondo romano dalle origini alla fine della Repubblica* , Giappichelli, Torino-Cuneo, 1955.

Fiandaca, G., *Prospettive possibili di maggiore tutela penale degli animali*, in *Per un codice degli animali*, Giuffrè, Milano, 2001.

Fox, Michael Allen, *Deep Vegetarianism*, Temple University Press, Philadelphia, 1999.

Francione, Gary, *Animals as Persons: essays on the abolition of animal exploitation*, Columbia University Press, New York, 2008.

Francione, Gary, *Animals, Property, and the Law*, Temple University Press, Philadelphia, VA, 1995.

Fuso, Silvano, *I nemici della scienza*, Edizioni Dedalo, Bari, 2009.

Giangrieco Pessi, Maria Vittoria, *Ricerche sull'actio de pauperie: dalle XII Tavole ad Ulpiano*, Jovene, Napoli, 1995.

Giovetti Paola, *I viaggi dell'anima,* Armenia, Milano, 1989.

Goldberg, Bruce, *Vite passate, vite future*, Armenia Editore, Milano, 1992.

Grand Rabbin Guigui, Albert, *Dieu parle aux hommes*, Editions Racine, Bruxelles, Belgio, 2007.

Greenhouse gas emissions from the dairy sector, FAO 2010.

Gregory, N.G., Grandin, T., *Animal Welfare and Meat Production*, CABI, Cambridge, 2007.

Hauser, Marc. D., *Menti morali*, Il Saggiatore, Milano, 2007.

Hawking, Stephen, *Dal Big-bang ai buchi neri – breve storia del tempo*, Rizzoli, Milano, 1988.

Hendrickson, Mary and William Heffernan. Concentration of Agricultural Markets, Department of Rural Sociology, University of Missouri, April 2007.

Hengelardt Jr., Hugo Tristram, *The Foundations of Bioethics*, 2nd edition, Oxford University Press, 1996.

Hoogenkamp, Henk W., *Soy protein and formulated meat products*, CABI, Cambridge, 2005.

Hublin, J.J, Richards, M.P., *The Evolution of Hominin Diets*, Springer B.V., Olanda, 2009.

Hui, Y. H., Nip, W.K., Rogers, R. W., *Meat Science and Applications* , Marcel Dekker, NY, 2005.

Ignatieff, Michael, *Human Right as Politics and Idolatry*, Princeton University Press, 2001,

Isnardi Parente, Margherita, *Le Tu ne tueras pas de Xénocrate, in A la mémoire de V. Goldschmidt*, Parigi (Francia), 1985.

Jagot, P.C., *Magnetismo e suggestione*, (trad. Emilio De Paoli) Siad, Milano, 1983.

Jain, Arun, *Be a vegetarian*, Kalpaz Publications, Delhi, 2008.

Johnson, Bettye, *I segreti rivelati nei rotoli di Maria Maddalena*, Macro Edizioni, Cesena, 2006.

Kaimowitz, Mertens, Wunder, Pacheco, *Hamburger Connection Fuels Amazon Destruction*, CIFOR, Center for International Forestry Research, 2003.

Kant, Immanuel, *Groundworks of the Metaphysics of Morals,* 2nd edition, Cambridge University Press, 2012.

Kaplan, David M., *The Philosophy of Food*, University of Calilfornia Press, 2012.

Kellogg, John Harvey, *New Dietetics: a guide to scientific feeding in health and disease*, Washington, 1923.

Kenner, Robert, *Food Inc.*, movie, Magnolia Pictures, 2008.

Leadbeater, Charles W., Vegetarianism and Occultism, Cosimo Inc., New York, 2007.

Leitzmann, Claus, *Vegetariani. Fondamenti, vantaggi e rischi*, Paravia Bruno Mondadori Editori, Milano, 2002.

Leitzmann, Claus, *Vegetariani. Fondamenti, vantaggi e rischi*, Paravia Bruno Mondadori Editori, Milano, 2002.

Lenoir, Frèdèric, *Piccolo trattato di storia delle religioni*, trad. a cura di: Emanuele Lana, Garzanti, Milano, 2011.

Lev Tolstoj, *Contro la caccia e il mangiar carne*, a cura di Gino Ditali, Isonomia editrice, 1994.

Levitico, nuova versione, introduzione e commento di Giovanni Deiana, Paoline Editoriale Libri, Milano, 2005.

Locke, John, *Secondo trattato sul governo*, II, 4, Rizzoli, Milano, 1998.

Lodovici, G.S., *L'utilità del bene. Jeremy Bentham, l'utilitarismo e il consequenzialismo*, Vita e Pensiero, Milano, 2004.

Lucarelli, Rita, *Il Libro dei Morti dall'Epoca Faraonica all'epoca Greco-Romana*, in "*Atene e Roma*", n. 3-4/2008.

Lugaresi, Nicola, Bertazzo, Silvia, *Nuovo codice dell'ambiente*, Maggioli Editore, Sant'Arcangelo di Romagna, 2009.

Luzzati, Claudio, *Questo non è un manuale – Percorsi di filosofia del diritto: 1*, Giappichelli, Torino, 2010.

Mannucci, Anna, *Animali e diritto italiano: una storia,* in *Per un codice degli animali*, Giuffrè, Milano, 2001.

Mannucci, Erica Joy, *La cena di Pitagora. Storia del vegetarianismo dall'antica Grecia a Internet*, Carocci editore, Roma, 2008.

Mansi M., Venturi B., Ughi E., *Tutto biologia*, De Agostini, Novara, 2005.

Marchi, Vittorio, *La scienza dell'Uno. La chiave dell'universo nascosto*, Macro Edizioni, Cesena, 2007.

Mariani Costantini, A. C. e altri, *Alimentazione e Nutrizione Umana*, Ed. Il pensiero scientifico, Roma, 2006.

Martines, Temistocle, *Diritto Costituzionale*, dodicesima edizione, Giuffrè editore, Milano, 2010.

Mason, Jim, Singer, Peter, *The Ethics of What We Eat*, Rodale, 2006.

Mattei, Rosalba, *Manuale di nutrizione clinica*, Franco Angeli, Milano, 2001.

Millar, West, Nerlich, *Ethical futures: bioscience and food horizons*, Wageningen Academic Publishers, Olanda, 2009.

Modenesi, Tamino, Verga, *Biotecnocrazia: informazione scientifica, agricoltura, decisione politica*, Edizione Jaca Book, Milano, 2007.

Momentè, Stefano, *Il veganismo. Una scelta di vita per gli animali, la salute e l'ambiente*, Xenia, Milano, 2011.

Montaigne, Michel de, *De la cruautè*, Edition Villey-Saulnier, Puf, Francia, 2004.

Montanari, Massimo, *Alimentazione e cultura nel Medioevo*, Laterza, Roma, 2008.

Montanari, Massimo, *Uomo e Ambiente nel mezzogiorno normanno-svevo*, Edizioni Dedalo, Bari, 1989.

Moore Lappé, Frances, *Diet for a small planet*, Ballantine Books, New York, 1982.

Morand S., Krasnov B.R., *The biogeography of host-parasite interactions*, Oxford University Press, New York, 2010.

More, Thomas, *Utopia: lo Stato perfetto ovvero l'isola che non c'è, traduzione e presentazione di Davide Sala*, Demetra, Bussolengo 1995.

Morghen, Raffaello, *Medioevo cristiano*, Laterza, Bari, 1994.

Myers, Norma, Kent, Jennifer, *Perverse Subsidies*, Island Press, Washington, D.C., 2001.

Myers, Norman, *The Hamburger Connection: how Central America's Forests Became North America's Hamburgers, Ambio*, vol. 10, n. 1, 1981, Royal Swedish Academy of Sciences.

Nestle, Eberhard, *Introduction to the Textual Criticism of the Greek Testament*, Williams & Norgate, 1901.

Nicholson, P.T., Shaw, Ian, *Ancient Egyptian Materials and Technology*, Cambridge University Press, 2000.

Onida, Pietro Paolo, *Studi sulla condizione degli animali non umani nel sistema giuridico romano*, Giappichelli, Torino, 2002.

P. Ovidio Nasone, *Metamorfosi, Libro 8-15*, Loescher, Novara, 2005.

Pallen, M.J., Nelson, K.E., Preston, G.M., *Bacterial Pathogenomics*, ASM Press, Washington D.C., 2007.

Philadelphia Committee, *History of the Philadelphia Bible-Christian Church for the First Century of its Existence: From 1817-1917*, General Books, Philadelphia, 2010.

Pinna, Sergio, *La protezione dell'ambiente. Il contributo della filosofia, dell'economia e della geografia*, Franco Angeli, Milano, 2003.

Pisanò, Attilio, *Diritti deumanizzati. Animali, ambiente, generazioni future, specie umana*, Giuffrè, Milano, 2012

Platania, Chiara, *Labirinti di gusto. Dalla cucina degli dei all'hamburger di McDonald*, Edizioni Dedalo srl, Bari, 2008.

Platone, *Le Leggi*, Rizzoli, Milano, 2005.

Plutarco , *Del mangiare carne* , Adelphi, Milano, 2001.

Pocar, Valerio, *Gli animali non umani*, Editori Laterza, Bari, 2005.

Quarta, Cosimo, *Una nuova etica per l'ambiente*, edizioni Dedalo, Bari, 2006.

Querini, Giulio, *La tutela dell'ambiente nell'Unione Europea: un'analisi critica*, Franco Angeli Editore, Milano, 2007.

Reale, Giovanni, *Invito al pensiero antico*, Editrice La Scuola, Brescia, 2011.

Regan, Tom, *Empty Cages: Facing the Challenge of Animal Rights*, Rowman & Littlefield, 2009.

Regan, Tom, *The Case for Animal Rights, University of California Press, 1983.*

Regan, Tom, *La mia lotta per i diritti animali*, Cosmopolis, Torino, 2005.

Rescigno, Francesca, *I diritti degli animali: da res a soggetti*, Giappichelli, Torino, 2005.

Resl, Brigitte, *A Cultural History of Animals in the Medieval Age*, Berg, New York, 2007.

Rousseau, Jean-Jacques, *Emile, ou de l'éducation*, Garnier Frères, Paris, 1866.

Ryder, R.D., *Victims of Science. The Use of Animals in Research*, London, Davis-Poynter, 1975.

Salima, Ikram, Divine Creatures: *Animal Mummies in Ancient Egypt*, The American University in Cairo Press, Egypt, 2005.

Salt, Henry S., *A plea for vegetarianism and other essays* , The vegetarian society, Macnhester, 1886.

Salt, Henry S., *Animals' Rights: Considered in Relation to Social Progress* , Macmillan & Co., 1894.

Santosuosso, A., *Autodeterminazione e diritto alla salute: da compagni di viaggio a difficili conviventi*, in *Notizie di Politeia*, 1997.

Scquizzato, Paolo, *Come un principio – Riflessioni sul libro della Genesi*, Effatà Editrice, Torino, 2010.

Seneca, *Tutte le opere* , by Giovanni Reale, Bompiani, Milano, 2000.

Sgrò, Renato Maria, *Sulle fonti dell'art. 727 del codice penale*, in Castignone – Battaglia, *I diritti degli animali*, Centro di bioetica di Genova, 1987.

Simonetti , Sergio , *L'anima in San* Tommaso *d'Aquino* , Armando, Roma 2007.

Singer, Peter, *Animal Liberation*, Harper Collins, 1975.

Singer, Peter, *Rethinking Life and Death*, St. Martin's Press, 1996.

Singh, U., *A History of Ancient and Medieval India: From the Stone Age to the 12 th Century*, Prentice Hall, New Jersey, 2009.

Spaemann, Robert, *Persons*, Oxford University Press, 2006.

Spagnolo, Massimo, *Elementi di economia e gestione della pesca*, Franco Angeli Editore, Milano, 2006.

Spurlock, Morgan, *Supersize me*, Kathbur Pictures, 2004.

Steinfeld, H., Mooney, H., Schneider, F., Neville, L., *Livestock in a changing landscape, Volume 1: Drivers, Consequences, and Responses*, SCOPE, Washington, 2010.

Stroppa, Claudio, *Cibo, società e scienza dell'alimentazione*, Aracne, Roma, 2007.

Stuart, Tristram, *The bloodless revolution*, W. & W. Norton Company Inc., New York, 2007.

Sukhotina-Tolstaia, T.L., *Tolstoy Remembered*, Joseph, London, 1977.

Taylor, Paul W., Respect for Nature, *A Theory of Environmental Ethics*, Princeton University Press, 1986.

Terence Scully, " *Tempering Medieval Food* " in *Food in the Middle Ages, ed* . Melitta Weiss Adamson, New York, 1995.

Toldrà, Fidel, Safety of meat and processed meat, Springer, New York, 2009.

Tonutti, Sabrina, *Diritti animali: storia e antropologia di un movimento*, Forum, Udine, 2007.

Torrente, Andrea, Schlesinger, Piero, *Manuale di diritto privato*, ventesima edizione, Giuffrè, Milano, 2011.

Trum Hunter, Beatrice, *Infectious Connections*, Basic Health Pubblications Inc., Laguna Beach, CA, 2009.

Ulpian, Digest, AD 530-533.

Vanderkam, James C., *The Dead Sea Scrolls Today,* W. B. Eerdmans Publishing Co., Grand Rapids, 1994.

Varner, Gary E., *Personhood, Ethics, and Animal Cognition: Situating Animals in Hare's Two-Level Utilitarianism*, Oxford University Press, 2012.

Vegetarian Times, n. 97, september, 1985.

Veronesi, Umberto, *Verso la scelta vegetariana. Il tumore si previene anche a tavola, Giunti Editore*, Firenze, 2012.

Visetti, Giampaolo, *Ex Italia Viaggio nel Paese che non sa più chi è*, Baldini e Castoldi Editore, Milano, 2009.

Voltaire, Elements de la Philosophie de Newton , 1741.

Voltaire, *Trattato sulla tolleranza*, trad. a cura di Lorenzo Bianchi, Feltrinelli Editore Milano, 2004.

Waldron A., Longworth J,W, Zhang, C.G., *China's livestock revolution: agribusiness and policy developments in the sheep meat industry*, CAB International, Cambridge, 2007.

Walker Bynum, Caroline, *Holy feast and holy fast. The religious significance of food to medieval women*, University of California Press, 1987.

Wambach, Helen, *Rivivere le vite passate*, Edizioni Mediterranee, Roma, 1993.

Weiss, Brian, *Molte vite, un'anima sola, Il potere di guarigione delle vite future e la terapia della progressione*, Mondadori, Milano, 2008.

Wise, Robert, *The Day the Earth Stood Still*, movie, Twentieth Century Fox, 1951.

Wolfgang Schirmacher, *Etica quotidiana. Schopenhauer e una mistica che parte dall'esperienza*, in Discipline Filosofiche 2/1994, Bologna, 1995.

World Bank. 2010. *World Development Report 2010 : Development and Climate Change*. Washington, DC. https://openknowledge.worldbank.org/handle/10986/4387 License: CC BY 3.0 IGO.

Sitography

A.F.P., *Vegetarians Barred from Adopting*, ABC, www.abc.net.au/news/2011-03-11/vegetarians-barred-from-adopting/2660904 (last consultation on 12/10/2012)

A.U., *Allarme inquinamento spaziale*, Geologi.info, www.geologi.info/Allarme-inquinamento-spaziale_news_x_9617.html (last consultation on 12/10/2012)

Amazon Destruction, CIFOR, www.cifor.org/publications/pdf_files/media/Amazon.pdf (last consultation on 12/10/2012)

Axon, W.E.A., *A Forerunner of the Vegetarian Society*, International Vegetarian Union, www.ivu.org/history/societies/britfor.html (last consultation on 12/10/2012)

Bartholet, Jeffrey, *When Will Scientists Grow Meat in a Petri Dish?*, Scientific American, www.scientificamerican.com/article.cfm?id=inside-the-meat-lab (last consultation on 12/10/2012)

Berizzi, Paolo, *Bambini in casa-famiglia, un business da un miliardo all'anno*, La Repubblica, www.repubblica.it/cronaca/2011/04/29/news/inchiesta_italiana-15507476/ (last consultation on 12/10/2012)

Beydoun, M.A., Wang, Y., *Meat consumption is associated with obesity and central obesity among US adults*, National Center for Biotechnology Information, www.ncbi.nlm.nih.gov/pmc/articles/P MC2697260/?tool=pubmed (last consultation on 12/10/2012)

Beyond Meat, beyondmeat.com/about/ (last consultation on 12/10/2012)

Buonaiuto, Alfonso Emiliano, Animali in tribunale, Jurisnews, jurisnews.wordpress.com/2009/09/30/animali-in-tribunale/ (last consultation on 12/10/2012)

Catechismo della Chiesa Cattolica, Vaticano, www.vatican.va/archive/catechism_it / p3s2c2a7_it.htm (last consultation on 12/10/2012)

Cattolici Vegetariani, www.cattolicivegetariani.it (last consultation on 12/10/2012)

Convenzione europea sugli animali da macello, Council of Europe, conventions.coe.int/Treaty/ita/Treaties/Html/102.htm (last consultation on 12/10/2012)

Corsini, Pierluigi, *Il consumo di carburante quale metodo di misura dello sforzo di pesca*, ASCOMAC, www.ascomac.it/sezionet/files/IL%20CONSUMO%20DI%20CARBURANTE.pdf (last consultation on 12/10/2012)

Craig, W. J, Mangels, A.R., *Position of the American Dietetic Association: Vegetarian Diets*, ADA, www.vrg.org/nutrition/ 2009_ADA_position_paper.pdf (last consultation on 12/10/2012)

Cruel and Improper Treatment of Cattle Act to Prevent the Cruel and Improper Treatment of Cattle, Animal rights History, www.animalrightshistory.org/animal-rights-law/romantic-legislation/1822-uk-act-ill-treatment-cattle.htm (last consultation on 12/10/2012)

Cruelty to Animals Act, 1835, Animal rights History, www.animalrightshistory.org/animal-rights-law/romantic-legislation/1835-uk-act-cruelty-to-animals.htm (last consultation on 12/10/2012)

Davies, *R.W.D.*, Cripps, S.J., Nickson, A., Porter, G., *Defining and estimating global marine fisheries bycatch* assets.panda.org/downloads/bycatch_paper.pdf (last consultation on 12/10/2012)

De Bac, Margherita, *Le epidemie mancate*, Corriere della Sera, www.corriere.it/cronache/08_marzo_03/epidemie_mancate_a43d7570-e8e9-11dc-9255-0003ba99c667.shtml (last consultation on 12/10/2012)

Decreto Ministeriale 21/9/11, Ministero dell'ambiente, www.dsa.minambiente.it/gpp/file/GU_21-09-2011_dm_all1.pdf (last consultation on 12/10/2012)

Dietary Guidelines for Americans, USA Health Department, health.gov/dietaryguidelines/ (last consultation on 12/10/2012)

Dizionario della lingua italiana del Corriere della sera, dizionari.corriere.it/dizionario _italiano/D/diritto_2.shtml (last consultation on 12/10/2012)

Dominiczak, Peter, *Social Workers Said No Meat No Diary Diet Was Starving Our Three Year Old Son*, This is London, www.thisislondon.co.uk/standard/article-23825755-social-workers-said-no-meat-no-dairy-diet-was-starving-our-three-year-old-son.do (last consultation on 12/10/2012)

Dossier LAV, *I costi reali della carne*, Lega Anti Vivisezione, www.lav.it/uploads/84/42404_dossier_LAV_ Costi_della_carne_vers.bassa_.pdf (last consultation on 12/10/2012)

DPR 320/54, Ministero della Salute, www.salute.gov.it/imgs/C_17_normativa_925_alle gato.pdf (last consultation on 12/10/2012)

Encefalopatie spongiformi trasmissibili, Ministero della salute, www.salute.gov.it/imgs/C_17_pagineAree_1558_listaFile_itemName_6_file.pdf (last consultation on 12/10/2012)

Farm Practices and Management of Fertilizer Use, United States Department of Agricolture, www.ers.usda.gov/ browse/view.aspx? subject=FarmPracticesManagementFertilizerUse (last consultation on 12/10/2012)

Farmaci: gelatine animali nei medicinali per pazienti vegetariani, Libero, www.liberoquotidiano.it/news/945155/Farmaci-gelatine-animali-nei-medicinali-per-pazienti-vegetariani-----.html (last consultation on 12/10/2012)

Fox, T. e Humphreys, B, *1847-1997 Vegetarianismo. Un motivo per festeggiare*, European Vegetarian Union, www.euroveg.eu/evu/italian/news/news972/celebrations.html (last consultation on 12/10/2012)

Frequently Asked Questions, Meat Abolition, www.meat-abolition.org/nl/content/frequently-asked-questions (last consultation on 12/10/2012)

Galline Ovaiole, Dossier della Lega Anti Vivisezione, www.lav.it/index.php?id=384 (last consultation on 12/10/2012)

Gemma, Gladio, *Costituzione e tutela degli animali*, 27/4/04, Forum di Quaderni Costituzionali, http://www.forumcostituzionale.it/site/images/stories/pdf/old_pdf/803.pdf (last consultation on 12/10/2012)

Giorgi, Elisabetta, *Una legge nazista vuole prendere mia figlia*, Il Tirreno, iltirreno.gelocal.it/regione/2012/01/31/news/una-legge-nazista-vuole-prendere-la-mia-jasmin-1.3127700 (last consultation on 12/10/2012)

History of The Vegetarian Society, Vegetarian Society, www.vegsoc.org/page.aspx?pid=827 (last consultation on 12/10/2012)

Isaac Bashevis Singer, International Vegetarian Union, www.ivu.org/history/northam 20b/singer.html (last consultation on 12/10/2012)

Kaimowitz, D., Mertens, B., Wunder S., Pacheco P., *Hamburger Connection Fuels* (last consultation on 12/10/2012)

La pesca del tonno, Greenpeace, www.greenpeace.org/raw/content/italy/ufficiostampa/file/scheda-tonni.pdf (last consultation on 12/10/2012)

La pesca nei mari di oggi, Eat-Ing, www.eat-ing.net/getpage.aspx?id=67&dx=2&m=2&pf =f&sez=pesce (last consultation on 12/10/2012)

LAV: Carne non indispensabile per i bambini, Mellin sospende lo spot tv, Prima Comunicazione, www.primaonline.it/2011/12/13/99072/lav-carne-non-indispensabile-per-bambini-mellin-sospende-lo-spot-tv/ (last consultation on 12/10/2012)

Legge 281/91, Ministero della salute, www.salute.gov.it/imgs/C_17_normativa_911_allegato.pdf

Legge 623/85, Normativa sanitaria, www.normativasanitaria.it/jsp/dettaglio.jsp?aggiorna menti=&id=26262&page=&posArt=1&articolo=1&subart =1&progr=1&anno=null (last consultation on 12/10/2012)

Legge n. 189/04, Camera dei Deputati Italiana, www.camera.it/parlam/leggi/04189l.htm (last consultation on 12/10/2012)

Lin, Doris, *McDonald's French Fries Still Not Vegetarian*, About.Com Animal rights, animalrights.about.com/b/2011/10/26/mcdonalds-french-fries-still-not-vegetarian.htm (last consultation on 12/10/2012)

Linee di indirizzo nazionale per la ristorazione scolastica, 2010, Ministero della salute, www.salute.gov.it/imgs/C_17_pubblicazioni_1248_allegato.pdf (last consultation on 12/10/2012)

Livestock Impact on Environment, FAO, www.fao.org/ag/magazine/0612sp1.htm (last consultation on 12/10/2012)

Malattia di Creutzfeldt-Jakob: che cos'è, editoriale, Osservatorio delle malattie rare, www.osservatoriomalattierare.it/index.php/component/content/article/38-sezioni/975-che-cose-la-malattia-di-creutzfeldt-jakob (last consultation on 12/10/2012)

Mannucci, Anna, *Animali e diritto italiano: una storia*, Osservatorio delle libertà ed istituzioni religiose, www.olir.it/areetematiche/42/documents/mannucci_animaliediritto.pdf (last consultation on 12/10/2012)

Martin's Act, 1822, Wikisource, en.wikisource.org/wiki/Martin's_Act_1822 (last consultation on 12/10/2012)

Martorelli, Stefania, *La dieta dei Neandertal*, Nationalgeographic, www.nationalgeographic.it/scienza/2011/03/22/news/la_dieta_dei_neandertal-246243/ (last consultation on 12/10/2012)

McDonald's Class Notice, Edelman, Combs, Latturner & Goodwin, www.edcombs.com/CM/Notices/Notices168.asp (last consultation on 12/10/2012)

McDonald's Lawsuit: What's The Story? Compassionate Spirit, www.compassionatespirit.com/ McDonalds-Lawsuit-article.htm (last consultation on 12/10/2012)

McDonald's Second Amended Complaint, Edelman, Combs, Latturner & Goodwin, www.edcombs.com/CM/Notices/Notices166.asp (last consultation on 12/10/2012)

Mekonnen, M.M., Hoekstra, A.Y., *The green, blue and grey water footprint of farm animals and animal products*, Waterfootprint, www.waterfootprint.org/Reports/Report-48-WaterFootprint-AnimalProducts-Vol1.pdf (last consultation on 12/10/2012)

Ministero della Sanità, Ordinanza 17/11/00, www.sanita.it/bse_gestione/login/Documenti/14-OM17-11-2000.pdf (last consultation on 12/10/2012)

Mucca pazza, due anni di paura, La Repubblica, www.repubblica.it/online/cultura_ scienze/mucca/pazza/pazza.html (last consultation on 12/10/2012)

Mucche a terra, Lega Anti Vivisezione, www.lav.it/index.php?id=430 (last consultation on 12/10/2012)

Murphy, Pat, Compulsive gambler rolls snake eyes in Mirapex suit Lawyers Usa Online, lawyersusaonline.com/benchmarks/ 2011/07/ (last consultation on 12/10/2012)

Ottica geometrica, dispensa, Università degli Studi di Siena, www.unisi.it/fisica/dip/dida/matinfef/ottica_geometrica.pdf (last consultation on 12/10/2012)

Otto, Stephan H., *Animal Protection Laws of the United States of America and Canada*, sixth edition, Animal Legal Defense Fund, aldf.org/downloads/APL6E-CA.pdf (last consultation on 12/10/2012)

Pasto fuori casa, incubo per i vegetariani, ANSA, wwww.ansa.it/saluteebenessere/notizie/rubriche/alimentazione/2011/08/01/visualizza_new.html_760041053.html (last consultation on 12/10/2012)

Peta offers $ 1 Million Reward to First to Make in Vitro Meat, PETA, www.peta.org/features/In-Vitro-Meat-Contest.aspx (last consultation on 12/10/2012)

Polli, Lega Anti Vivisezione, www.lav.it/index.php?id=382 (last consultation on 12/10/2012)

Pollution from fishing vessels, Australian Maritime Safety Authority, www.amsa.gov.au/ma-rine_environment_protection/Protection_of_Pollution_from_Ships/Pollution_from_Fishi ng_Vessels.asp (last consultation on 12/10/2012)

Q&A: Reform of EU Farm Policy, BBC News Europe, news.bbc.co.uk/2/hi/ 4407792.stm#howspent (last consultation on 12/10/2012)

Report Economico-Finanziario 2010, ISMEA, www.ismea.it/flex/cm/pages/ServeAttach-ment.php /L/IT/D/1%252F9%252F3%252FD.27a8b0003f65979d041d/P/BLOB%3AID%3 D5388 (last consultation on 12/10/2012)

Rossi, M., *Il vegetariano pentito, la carne fa bene al pianeta*, Tuttogreen, www.tuttogreen.it/il-vegetariano-pentito-la-carne-fa-bene-al-pianeta/ (last consultation on 12/10/2012)

Rovito, Cristian, *L'inquinamento atmosferico provocato dalle navi: analisi e approfondimento della connessa normativa internazionale e comunitaria*, Diritto all'Ambiente, www.simoline.com/clienti/dirittoambiente/file/acque_marino_40.pdf (last consultation on 12/10/2012)

Ryder, Richard, *Speciesism*, Dr. Richard Ryder UK, www.richardryder.co.uk/speciesism.html (last consultation on 12/10/2012)

Sala, A., Lucchetti, A., Ferretti, M., Mariani, A., Serra, S., *Rapporto finale indagine prelimi-nare dell'impatto sul fondale marino esercitato dalla pesca con reti a strascico gemelle e prime valutazioni dell'efficienza di pesca*, Regione Abruzzo, www.regione.abruzzo.it/pesca/ docs/fupDocumentazione/Punto_4_OdG_studio_reti_americane.pdf (last consultation on 12/10/2012)

Salt, Henry, *A Plea for Vegetarianism*, International Vegetarian Union, www.ivu.org/history/ europe19b/salt_a_plea_for_vegetarianism.pdf (last consultation on 12/10/2012)

Santese, Giuseppina, *Vegetariani e filosofi nel mondo antico*: www.fondazionebasso.it/site/_ files/Risorse_on_line/Parole_chiave/disobbedienza/santesecorretto.doc (last consultation on 12/10/2012)

Should The Animals be Used For Scientific Research? Focusing on Agricultural Issues, web.ics.purdue.edu/~peters/HTML/issues/animal-examples.html (last consultation on 12/ 10/2012)

Si fa presto a dire foto, Focus, www.focus.it/scienza/775_19042008_Tecniche_ fotogra-fiche_C9.aspx (last consultation on 12/10/2012)

Stop a campagne contro carne e pellicce per difendere il made in Italy, ADN Kronos, www.adnkronos.com/IGN/Sostenibilita/Risorse/Stop-a-campagne-contro-carne-e-pellicce-per-dife ndere-il-Made-in-Italy_312929951103.html (last consultation on 12/10/2012)

Tabella Bufalini, ISMEA, www.ismea.it/flex/cm/pages/ServeAttachment.php/L/IT/D/ 3%252F2 %252F8%252FD.0f10c04239a29df5422c/P/BLOB%3AID%3D6631 (last con-sultation on 12/10/2012)

Tettamanti, M., *Valutazione di impatto ambientale di un anno di caccia in Italia, Vittime della caccia*, www.vittimedellacaccia.org/pdf/RelazioneImpattoAmbientalePiombo.pdf (last con-sultation on 12/10/2012)

The Doctrine and Covenants, The Church of Jesus Christ of Latter-Day Saints, lds.org/scrip-tures/dc-testament/dc/89?lang=eng (last consultation on 12/10/2012)

The Healthian, editoriale, International Vegetarian Union, www.ivu.org/history/england19a/ healthian.pdf (last consultation on 12/10/2012)

The Vegan News, The Vegan Society, Watson, D., www.vegansociety.com/uploadedFiles/ About_The_Society/Publications/The_Vegan_magazine/Feature_Articles/1944-news.pdf (last consultation on 12/10/2012)

Trapianto di viso, la donna non fu aggredita, Corriere della sera, www.corriere.it/Primo_Piano/ Cronache/2005/12_Dicembre/02/cane.shtml (last consultation on 12/10/2012)

Trattato di Lisbona, Consiglio dell'Unione Europea, www.consilium.europa.eu/treaty-of-lis-bon?lang=it (last consultation on 12/10/2012)

Tribunale tedesco affida la bimba al papà la mamma si barrica in casa con la bimba, La Repubblica, firenze.repubblica.it/cronaca/2012/01/12/news/il_tribunale_tedesco_affida_bi mba_a_ pap_la_mamma_si_ barrica_in_casa_con_la_bimba-28013026/ (last consultation on 12/10/2012)

Vallejo Rodriguez, Luis, *Omnivorous or Vegetarian? European Vegetarian Union*, www.euroveg.eu/evu/english/news/news962/omnivore.html (last consultation on 12/10/2012)

Vegan Society, la storia, www.vegansociety.com/about/history.aspx (last consultation on 12/10/2012)

Verein Gegen Tierfabriken, The Abolitionist Approach, www.abolitionistapproach.com/media/links/p140/essay.pdf (last consultation on 12/10/2012)

Weiss, B., *People Often Ask*, Brian Weiss www.brianweiss.com/ask_me.html (last consultation on 12/10/2012)